The Art of French
Beaded Flowers

Creative Techniques for Making 30 Beautiful Blooms

The Art of French Beaded Flowers

Creative Techniques for Making 30 Beautiful Blooms

Carol Benner Doelp

LARK BOOKS

A Division of Sterling Publishing Co., Inc.
New York

To Ruth and Ralph,
my fairy godparents

EDITOR
Marcianne Miller

ART DIRECTOR
Stacey Budge

PHOTOGRAPHER
Keith Wright

COVER DESIGNER
Barbara Zaretsky

ILLUSTRATOR
Orrin Lundgren

ASSISTANT EDITOR
Nathalie Mornu

ASSOCIATE ART DIRECTORS
Lance Wille
Shannon Yokeley

EDITORIAL ASSISTANCE
Delores Gosnell
Anne Hollyfield

EDITORIAL INTERN
Kalin Siegwald

Library of Congress Cataloging-in-Publication Data

Doelp, Carol Benner.
  The art of French beaded flowers : creative techniques for making 30
beautiful blooms / Carol Benner Doelp.— 1st ed.
      p. cm.
Includes index.
  ISBN 1-57990-426-2
  1. Bead flowers. I. Title.
  TT890.2.D64 2004
  745.58'2—dc22
                                                        2003015807
10 9 8 7 6 5 4 3 2 1

First Edition

Published by Lark Books, a division of
Sterling Publishing Co., Inc.
387 Park Avenue South, New York, N.Y. 10016

© 2004, Carol Benner Doelp

Distributed in Canada by Sterling Publishing,
c/o Canadian Manda Group, One Atlantic Ave., Suite 105
Toronto, Ontario, Canada M6K 3E7

Distributed in the U.K. by Guild of Master Craftsman Publications Ltd., Castle Place,
166 High Street, Lewes, East Sussex, England
BN7 1XU
Tel: (+ 44) 1273 477374, Fax: (+ 44) 1273 478606, Email: pubs@thegmcgroup.com,
Web: www.gmcpublications.com

Distributed in Australia by Capricorn Link (Australia) Pty Ltd.,
P.O. Box 704, Windsor, NSW 2756 Australia

If you have questions or comments about this book, please contact:
Lark Books
67 Broadway
Asheville, NC 28801
(828) 253-0467
Printed in China

ISBN: 1-57990-426-2

Foreword

I am delighted that in these first years of the 21st century, French flower beading is back in style, and that so many crafters are enjoying both my patterns and the newer ones that have been created today. It gives me great pleasure to know that artisans like Carol Benner Doelp are both teaching and writing books in order to share with others the techniques of the craft I have so enjoyed. To all of you who pick up this book I wish you well, and Happy Beading!

—*Virginia Nathanson*
Long Island, NY
Author of The Art of Making
　　Bead Flowers and Bouquets

Table of Contents

Introduction

One of the most frequent reactions from people who first see a bouquet of beaded flowers is, "Oh, I could never do that." Not true! Making French beaded flowers is an art that anyone can practice. It requires little investment in tools and materials, and no special skills. If you follow the directions in this book, you'll soon be making beautiful beaded flowers that will satisfy your creativity, decorate your home, and utterly delight all the lucky people who receive them as gifts.

This craft is extremely accessible, even if you have no previous beading or craft experience. Perhaps the best proof of that is my own story. I am a career bureaucrat; my educational background is in public health, not art. I had always thought of myself as a left-brain type, without an artistic or creative bone in my body. Until I found beads…

In 1991 at Christmastime, my oldest sister, an artist, gave me a beautiful beaded necklace she made. I wore it so often that after a few months the clasp broke. Since I couldn't return it for repairs, I decided to fix it myself. I took a jewelry class at the local bead store, fixed the necklace, then took another class, and another, and another—I was hooked!

Beads brought out something new in me. They are pretty just by themselves, but when you string them together, they become more than just a collection of beads—they take on a life all their own. They are enticing, alluring, magical, fantastic! A display of unstrung beads is a universe of unlimited creative possibilities.

Searching for beads, touching them, and combining them into woven necklaces and other pieces of jewelry became an artistic pleasure unlike anything I had experienced before. Instead of multitasking—surfing the net, watching TV, and talking on the telephone all at the same time—suddenly I was working happily for hours on end with my beads, being peaceful and calm. As all beaders come to know, beads are the perfect relaxation therapy.

When my brother became engaged, I decided to make a beaded corsage for his bride and a boutonniere for him. I looked everywhere for books to tell me how to make the flowers, finding only a series of out-of-print books. But from those few vintage sources, I realized that by putting beads on wire and bending the wire, I could create all kinds of dazzling flowers.

The roses I made for my brother's wedding were a hit, and suddenly I had not just a hobby but a calling. I made a gold beaded rose for a friend's wedding bouquet. When another friend was ill, I delivered beaded posies to brighten her day, and when a special coworker moved to a new job, I made my own version of a Japanese iris to say "thank you

I LEARNED MUCH ABOUT FRENCH BEADED FLOWERS BY STUDYING VINTAGE FLOWERS I FOUND IN ANTIQUE SHOPS.

and farewell." Just as my mother-in-law once made cakes to give to friends on special occasions, I was now doing the same with beaded flowers.

When I learned about *immortelles,* the elaborate beaded mourning wreaths from the Victorian era, I began to collect them, as well as vintage books on beaded flowers. I searched intently for one particular book written by Virginia Nathanson, the grande dame of French beaded flowers in the late 1960s. I discovered Mrs. Nathanson's whereabouts, phoned her, and asked if she had any books for sale. She had one left, she said, and sold it to me for $8.95, the 1969 cover price!

My friendship with Mrs. Nathanson has been nothing less than inspirational.

Following her example, I began to teach French beaded flower making. What a delight it's been to see the smiles of so many students when, at the end of a long day, they've completed beautiful beaded bouquets. The extension of my joy in their accomplishment has been the writing of this book. *The Art of French Beaded Flowers* is a dream come true—the chance to extend my teaching by sharing my favorite French beaded flower patterns and the techniques I've learned for making them.

May you enjoy reading this book as much as I enjoyed putting it together and may you, too, share with others the love of this beautiful craft.

SIMPLE ROSES WERE THE FIRST BEADED FLOWERS I MADE.

History of French Beaded Flowers

THE ART OF FRENCH BEADED FLOWERS REACHED ITS ZENITH IN THE ELABORATE MOURNING WREATHS OF THE VICTORIAN ERA.

As with many other expressions of folk art, the evolution of the French beaded flower technique is not well documented. The European peasants who apparently developed the craft were at best only marginally literate, and very little was written down. Instead the techniques were taught and handed down from one generation to the next, and their origins became obscured over time.

This much we do know: the French beaded flower technique developed over several centuries and it was not exclusively French. The distinguishing characteristic of the French technique is its simplicity. The beads are strung on wire, not woven, and the beaded wires are twisted into four basic patterns, which become the component parts of a finished flower. Unlike the beaded flower method known as Victorian, in which the wire may go through the beads twice, in French beaded flowers the wire goes through the bead only once.

The beads themselves, known as *rocailles,* were produced mostly in Italy, and examples of the flower-making technique can be found in Italy and in England, as well as in France. During the 19th century, beads were much in vogue as embellishments for ball gowns and other intricate formal wear. The frugal workers who painstakingly sewed or wove the beads onto clothing saved for themselves the beads that either wouldn't fit on the needles or were broken or irregular. From the salvaged beads, they strung the beads onto a single wire, bending the wire into flower shapes to decorate tables and church altars.

The Victorians were responsible for bringing about the zenith of the art of French beaded flowers. Their elaborate rituals of mourning, inspired by Queen Victoria's grief over the loss of her beloved Prince Albert, extended well beyond traditional funerals. Tokens of mourning took many artistic expressions, including collages that held small personal possessions and a lock of the deceased's hair. Visits to the beloved's gravesite were frequent. Then as now, flowers were laid in tribute, but in those days flowers were available only in season. At some time during the era, women began to assemble French beaded flowers into mourning wreaths.

The glass-beaded wreaths had several advantages over fresh flowers: they were less expensive, they were available all year round, and they were extremely durable. The wreaths, and eventually most other sorts of commemorative funeral art, came to be known as *immortelles*— a name that may reflect the everlasting nature of the ornaments, or they may simply have been named after the immortelle, a long-lasting flower native to southern Europe.

In the United States, immortelles came into widespread use in Louisiana, where French influence was strong. *Godey's Ladies Magazine*, a popular publication in the 1800s, occasionally showed patterns for French beaded flowers, which suggests that the flowers were also used for decorations besides those connected with mourning.

Some of the wreaths and older flowers can still be found in antique shops or on Internet auctions. When you look at these vintage wreaths, it's easy to see the four shapes that are the fundamental components of all French beaded flowers—the three different loop techniques and the basic frame, which you'll learn in the pages that follow.

The French techniques were resurrected in the 1930s when flowers were made and exported from France and Italy to American department stores. In magazines and fashion sales material from the time, you can find pictures of women sitting on the side of the street making flowers from beads and wire.

In the mid-1960s, Virginia Nathanson, a former vaudeville performer and songstress, bought an arrangement of the flowers in a department store, took it apart at home, and figured out how to re-create the flowers. Using that single bouquet as a point of departure, she taught herself the craft and began to create her own patterns. Eventually she authored several books on the subject. French beaded flowers enjoyed widespread popularity at the time,

UNLIKE SILK FLOWERS, BEADED FLOWERS WERE NEVER RESTRICTED BY THE NEED TO BE BOTANICALLY CORRECT.

and several other women, including Ruth Wasley, Edith Harris, Bobbee Anderson, and Virginia Osterland, followed Mrs. Nathanson's path and began to develop patterns and write books of their own. A great number of the patterns that we use today are derived from the work begun by these women.

Nearly half a century later, we're experiencing another revival of interest in French beaded flowers. Creative people throughout the world, particularly in the United States, France, Italy, and Japan, are applying 21st-century materials and technology to this 19th-century art, and the results are spectacular. No longer are French beaded flowers confined to vases; they've become fashion accessories, designer jewelry, and accents for home and office. Commemorative beaded wreaths, updated from their Victorian predecessors, have again become popular.

Some flowers are faithful reproductions of their living counterparts; others are wild and gaily colored fantasies. These new creations share the same characteristics and advantages of the older originals—they are easily made using inexpensive materials and straightforward techniques. Simplicity and accessibility were the main attractions of this craft at its genesis; they are its hallmarks today.

THE DECADE OF "FLOWER POWER" SAW A REVIVAL OF THE ART OF FRENCH BEADED FLOWERS AND AN ENTHUSIASTIC EMBRACE OF A CHEERFULLY EXPANDED PALETTE.

THE PALETTE OF THE MOURNING WREATHS WAS BEAUTIFUL BUT SOMBER.

COMMEMORATIVE WREATHS ARE BACK IN STYLE. I MADE THIS ONE TO HONOR MY FATHER, LT. COL. JOHN A. BENNER.

Basics

IT NEVER CEASES TO AMAZE ME HOW MUCH BEAUTY CAN COME FROM THE SIMPLE PROCESS OF COMBINING BEADS AND WIRE.

Making French beaded flowers is a simple art, a combination of stringing beads on wire and sculpting them into shape by bending and molding them with your fingers. It's a passion that you can indulge just about anywhere—as a passenger in a car, waiting in the dentist's office, or relaxing at home accompanied by music or TV. The main materials, small colorful glass beads, are objects that are not only lovely to look at but also exciting to work with. The tools needed are few, the techniques easy to learn, and the resulting flower projects can last forever.

ABOUT FLOWERS

When you begin to make French beaded flowers, you become more observant of real flowers, appreciating their vast differences as well as the subtle nuances among individual species. You notice the number and shape of petals and leaves, peek underneath to see the details of a calyx and sepals, compare their fascinating centers. Mostly, your eyes come alive to the glory of color in flowers, that extraordinary attraction that reaches out to bees and other pollinators as much as it does to each of us, saying, "Wow, look at me! I'm beautiful!"

Although many of my flowers look like the real thing, my style is not to replicate flowers, but to create them as I perceive them. For example, I see a daffodil as big, yellow, and showy. I know that the leaf starts at the ground level, but I prefer to place it a bit higher up the stem so it can be bent over the top of the vase.

You, too, should feel free to modify nature to fit the artistic vision the beads inspire in you. Likewise, alter my flower patterns as you wish. If you want to add more or fewer stamens, or a crystal stamen in place of what I have suggested, go ahead. If you want to make a bright blue poppy when mine is red, or make a dozen flowers in a display where I've made only three, do it.

"Perfect flowers aren't perfect," I always remind my students. Once I made a basket of black-eyed Susans and took them to my floral teacher. Every petal was perfectly placed around the stem. The first thing my teacher did was gently bend the petals this way and that. I stood in disbelief—and then awe— at how my bouquet perked up and came alive. Feel free to give your flowers that same natural touch.

Throughout the book I use a few botanical terms relating to flowers. Knowing them not only lets us marvel at the wondrous structure of flowers but also provides a basis of comparison for all the beaded flowers we make.

PARTS OF A BEADED FLOWER

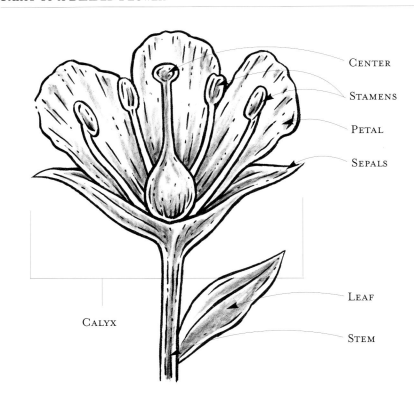

CENTER

STAMENS

PETAL

SEPALS

CALYX

LEAF

STEM

PETALS—tiny or giant, flat or curved, straight or ruffled, bunched or rayed, tubular or round—are the showiest parts of a flower.

LEAVES are usually green and are placed on a stem under the petals. In beaded flowers they can have round or pointed tops and bottoms.

CALYX is the green leaflike structure that covers a bud. After the bud blossoms, the calyx remains under the petals. A carnation has a well-defined calyx.

SEPALS are the leaflike components that make up the calyx. A rose, for example, has individual sepals.

STAMENS, which hold the pollen, are the male parts of the flower's reproductive system, located in the center. They can be clustered together (the black-eyed Susan), tall and grand (the tiger lily), or squiggly (the snapdragon)—or not visible at all, like the pistils, the female parts.

STEMS are the basic support of the flower, holding the leaves, sepals, calyx, and petals.

CENTER is a nonscientific term I use to describe any flower parts that are usually clustered in the middle of the blossom where all the petals come together.

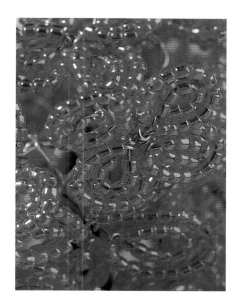

FLORETS are usually more than a petal but not quite a whole flower. Groups of florets are usually clustered together to form a blossom.

RACEME is a cluster of florets, usually hanging from a vine in a conelike shape.

BEADS

French beaded flowers are made with small glass beads, sometimes called rocailles, or seed beads. Now manufactured primarily in Japan and the Czech Republic, the beads come in a variety of sizes, colors, and finishes.

Seed beads have been manufactured since long before weights and measures became standardized, so size descriptions can sometimes be confusing. In general, the larger the number, the smaller the bead. The sizes range from very small, size 20/0, a bead so small you can hardly see it, to size 6/0, the size of a dried pea.

For beaded flowers, we most often use beads in the 9/0 to 12/0 range, with the occasional delicate flower using the tiny 15/0 bead. Most projects in this book use size 11/0 beads. The approximate number of hanks you'll need is listed in the instructions for each project. If you use a different size bead, you may, of course, need more or less hanks. In any case, you'll always want to have extra beads rather than too few.

FROM LARGEST TO SMALLEST, THESE ARE THE SIZES OF BEADS MOST OFTEN USED IN FRENCH BEADED FLOWERS. TOP ROW, LEFT TO RIGHT: 6/0, 8/0, 9/0. BOTTOM ROW, LEFT TO RIGHT: 11/0, 12/0, 15/0

BIGGER BEADS, INCLUDING CRYSTAL
BEADS, ARE SOMETIMES ADDED FOR A
DRAMATIC TOUCH ON SHOWY STAMENS.

Japanese beads are generally more
regularly shaped than Czech beads.
They have larger holes, and some
flower beaders find them easier to
work with. These beads are sold
loose, packaged in 10 to 20-gram
tubes or in ½-kilo bags.

Czech beads are threaded on
strands and sold as a group, or
hank, of beads. A hank of 11/0
beads usually includes twelve
20-inch strands (240 inches) and
is roughly equivalent to 50 grams
of Japanese loose beads. Because
of the irregularity of the beads, the
resulting flowers look more natural.
The Czech beads are also well
known for the faceted or cut edges
that make beaded flowers sparkle.

Making beaded flowers is bead
intensive and can be expensive,
so it's always best to purchase your
beads in bulk. I have a few basic

YOU CAN PURCHASE BEADS IN THREE WAYS: LOOSE, ON HANKS, OR IN TUBES.

colors—transparent red, green,
and yellow—that I use frequently.
I purchase these beads by the
½-kilo, saving money in the long
run. I add pizzazz to my bouquets
with the sparkly cut beads or color-
lined beads. Pink, purple, and blue
beads are hard to find, so I'm always
on the lookout for these.

TIP: If you see a bead you like, buy
three or four hanks, so you have at
least enough to complete one or
two flowers.

Bead Finishes

BEADS COME IN A VARIETY OF FINISHES, GIVING FLOWERS A WIDE RANGE OF TEXTURE AND SPECIAL EFFECTS.

1 Metallic beads: silver or gold finish

2 Color-lined beads: different color on the inside of the bead

3 Matte beads: flat finish, resembles etching

4 Opaque beads: solid, non-reflecting colors

5 Iris beads: multi-colored from tiny metallic particles

6 Luster beads: pearl-like sheen

7 Silver-lined beads: transparent with shiny silver interior

8 Transparent beads: see-through, most popular flower bead

9 Rainbow beads: multi-colored finish, soft and subtle

10 Cut beads: faceted and highly reflective, makes sparkling flowers

WIRE

While beads are the visible component of beaded flowers, it's wire that keeps the beads together, giving the flower structure. Craft wires come in a wide variety of colors, so it will be easy to match the wire with your beads. Like beads, the higher the number of the wire, the smaller it is. A 34-gauge wire is narrow in diameter and flexible; 16-gauge wire is thick and stiff.

When you start making beaded flowers, bending the wires may hurt your fingers. Be assured this won't last long—beaders are as proud of the calluses on their fingertips as guitar players are.

After a while you may want to use 24-gauge paddle wire instead of the 24-gauge craft wire. Although it's just as thick as craft wire, the paddle wire is stiffer and results in a structurally stronger leaf or petal. It's also less expensive than craft wire. You can find it with the floral supplies in a craft store.

Keep on hand a good supply of basic wire colors—gold, white, red, and green—which is generally all you need. For example, if you're using a black bead, the green wire will work just fine.

See the photo of the different flower-making wires on the next page.

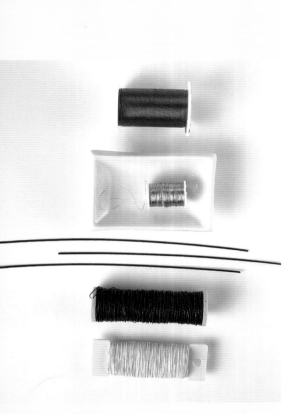

Flower-Making Wire

- 24 to 26-gauge colored wire is the most commonly used wire. Craft and bead stores carry the widest variety of colors.
- 30 to 34-gauge wire is used to assemble the flower (called "assembly" wire in the instructions), and in the lacing technique which strengthens certain parts.
- 18-gauge wires, usually in pairs and wrapped in floral tape, make most stems. They come in packages, found with floral supplies in craft stores. It's okay to use a single 16-gauge wire if you can find it. For heavier flowers, cut a length from a wire coat hanger.
- Paddle wire, usually 24 to 30-gauge, comes on spools...
- ...or wrapped on a "paddle."

THE BASIC FLOWER-MAKING KIT CONTAINS ALL THE SUPPLIES YOU NEED.

TOOLS & SUPPLIES

You don't need many tools for making beaded flowers, but you will need all of them as standard equipment for every project. Here's what to include in your Basic Flower-Making Kit.

- a pair of wire cutters to cut the wire
- flat-nose pliers and round-nose pliers to bend the wire
- nylon jaw-nose pliers to remove kinks from the wire
- selection of colored wires: 24 to 26-gauge
- assembly wire: 30 to 34-gauge
- stem wires: 18-gauge
- floral tape in green, brown, and white
- metal triangles to sort and scoop up loose beads
- small scissors
- tape measure or 6-inch ruler
- clear plastic bags to store loose beads and flower parts
- a bead spinner to string beads onto the wire
- silk or embroidery floss to wrap the stem
- glue to hold floss on stem
- tapestry needles for the lacing technique
- floral clay, dried moss, and marbles for planters and vases
- stiff coffee cup holders to store flowers

ONE REASON PEOPLE LOVE TO MAKE FRENCH BEADED FLOWERS IS THAT YOU CAN CARRY ALL THE NECESSARY SUPPLIES IN A LITTLE ZIPPERED POUCH!

PHOTO 1. TRANSFER PRESTRUNG BEADS DIRECTLY TO WIRE.

PHOTO 2. SCOOP LOOSE BEADS ONE AT A TIME ONTO THE WIRE.

PHOTO 3. USE A BEAD SPINNER TO QUICKLY STRING MANY BEADS.

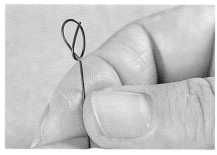

PHOTO 4. ALWAYS KNOT THE END OF THE WIRE.

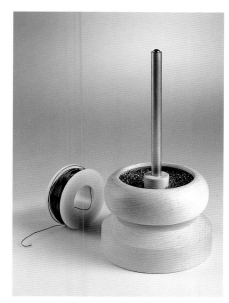

YOU CAN FIND BEAD SPINNERS, PLASTIC OR WOOD, IN BEAD OR CRAFT STORES AND ON THE INTERNET.

STRINGING THE BEADS

Before you start making a flower from a pattern, you'll string beads onto a wire that stays on its spool. It's important to have enough beaded wire on the spool so that you don't run out before you can complete the whole petal or leaf. The amount of beads and the length of wire you'll need will vary from flower to flower. You can put the beads on the wire as you make each part, or you can string several hanks onto the wire ahead of time.

There are three ways to string beads, and the method you use depends solely on your preference.

If the beads are prestrung on a hank, you can gently loosen one strand from the knot and transfer the beads directly from the thread to the wire. (See photo 1, upper right.)

If the beads are loose, you can place them in a small dish and use the end of the wire to scoop the beads onto the wire. (See photo 2 at right.)

A bead spinner offers another option. (See photo 3.) It's a two-part gadget: a base with a metal rod protruding from the center, and a wooden bowl that fits over the rod. I first saw one in a store in rural Maryland when the owner was using it to put loose beads on thread for knitting. I immediately bought one and started putting beads directly onto wire. All those hours I saved of stringing beads by hand—I thought I had died and gone to heaven!

Here's how it works. Fill the bowl with beads. With one hand, stick the end of the spool wire in the bowl slightly under the beads, and with the other hand, gently turn the bowl by turning the metal rod. Voilà!—the beads hop onto the wire.

Remember, when you're beading the wire, you'll also need bare wire to work with. Although the amount of bare wire will vary according to the instructions, the usual ratio of bare wire to beaded wire is about 1 to 3.

Always knot the end of the wire to keep the beads from falling off. (See photo 4.) If you're working with a short piece of wire, knot both ends. Fold about ½ inch of the wire into a loop and twist. Bend the tip of the wire up to keep from poking yourself.

TIP: In general, you can estimate the amount of beads you'll need for each part by looking at the project pattern and following the tips in Flower-Making Math on page 25.

STRIPING ADDS AN EXCITING DASH OF EXTRA COLOR.

TIPPING THE LOOPS ENHANCES THE APPEAL OF RUFFLED PETALS.

TIPPING THE EDGES GIVES DISTINCTION TO MULTI-PETALED FLOWERS.

SHADING AND USING COLOR

Single color flowers are beautiful; multicolored blooms are spectacular. The projects throughout the book feature a variety of ways to add both realism and whimsy to your flowers with the use of special coloring techniques.

OUTLINING WITH A CONTRASTING COLOR ADDS DRAMATIC FLAIR.

TWO DIFFERENT COLORS OF PETALS INTENSIFY THEIR SPARKLE.

SHADING CREATES REALISTIC COLORING.

SUPPLIES TO DISPLAY YOUR FLOWERS CAN BE FOUND IN THE FLORAL SECTION OF CRAFT STORES: DRIED MOSS, FLORAL CLAY, MARBLES, AND SIMPLE WIRE FORMS FOR WREATHS.

WHEN THE FLOWERS ARE ARRANGED AS PLANTS, USE A FLORAL CLAY BASE IN WHICH YOU INSERT THE STEM OF THE FLOWERS, AND COVER THE BASE WITH DRIED MOSS.

ASSEMBLING A FLOWER

After you make the parts of the flower, you'll assemble them into a complete flower. The assembly techniques you choose depend on what kind of stem you want.

For flowers that are used for pins, wreaths, and hair or clothing accessories, you can twist the wires from the center units or stamens to create a stem. See the Classic Poppy Pin on page 33—its assembly methods are similar to most other flowers with a short stem.

For long, sturdy stems, such as for flowers in vases or planters, you need to strengthen and stiffen the wires so they can hold the weight of the flower parts. Use 2 pieces of 18-gauge wire wrapped with floral tape; the tape provides a sticky surface and makes the assembly easier. If you need something stiffer, cut a wire coat hanger.

DISPLAYING YOUR BEADED FLOWERS

You can display beaded flowers in as many ways as you do real flowers. But remember that because they are glass, beaded flowers are heavy and need to be arranged solidly and attached securely. The taller the vase, the more likely it is to need added weight for security.

FOR A BOUQUET OF FLOWERS, CHOOSE A STURDY VASE AND ADD FLORAL MARBLES OR PEBBLES THAT WILL HELP ANCHOR THE STEMS AND KEEP THE FLOWERS FROM TIPPING OVER.

WHAT COULD BE A MORE PERFECT CONTAINER FOR A BOUQUET OF BEADED FLOWERS THAN A BEADED BASKET?

SMALL BEADED FLOWER ARRANGEMENTS ARE SUITABLE GIFTS FOR COWORKERS AND BUSINESS ASSOCIATES. MAKE MORE ELABORATE DISPLAYS FOR CLOSE FRIENDS AND FAMILY.

BEADED FLOWERS AS GIFTS

Your friends will be thrilled with your gifts of beaded flowers. However, they may not know how to care for them and would love a helpful reminder. Feel free to make copies of this sample gift card and include it with your flowers.

GETTING STARTED

In the next two chapters, you'll learn, step-by-step, how to use the four basic French beaded flower-making techniques to make your first project—the Classic Poppy Pin. Have fun!

Your Gift of French Beaded Flowers

ENJOY YOUR BEADED FLOWERS—NO SUN, NO WATER, AND NO FERTILIZER NEEDED!

- If the flowers get dusty, gently clean them with a soft-bristle brush, such as a pastry brush. Or use a tissue and glass cleaner to delicately clean each petal.

- If your flowers need a "washing," provide a gentle rain with a water faucet.

- Dry the flowers as soon as possible, either by patting dry with paper towels or with a hair dryer set on low.

- It's okay to put your flowers into a different vase. But remember the flowers are heavy-weight the new container with marbles or pebbles so it doesn't tip over.

- If the cat knocks over the arrangement, don't panic! Use your fingers to re-shape any parts that got disheveled, and put the flowers back on display.

IN A SHORT TIME, YOU'LL GAIN THE CONFIDENCE TO MAKE DISPLAYS WITH MANY PARTS.

Techniques

There are four basic beaded flower techniques—three are variations on making loops and the fourth is based on the model of a frame. Their names are descriptive: Continuous Loops, Continuous Crossover Loops, Continuous Wraparound Loops, and Basic Frame.

In this chapter, you'll find an overview of those basic techniques, with general descriptions that give you an idea of how the techniques relate to the flower-making process and to each other. In the first project that immediately follows, Classic Poppy Pin (page 33), you'll learn how to apply the fundamental methods to specific flower parts and combine them into a completed flower.

I strongly recommend you make the poppy as your first project because it will prepare you for making all the other flowers in this book.

IT'S MAGIC WHEN YOU TURN AN UNFORMED MASS OF TINY GLASS BEADS INTO AN EXQUISITE FLOWER.

SINCE THERE ARE ONLY FOUR BASIC
TECHNIQUES, IT DOESN'T TAKE LONG TO
LEARN HOW TO USE THE PATTERNS FOR
EACH ONE. IN AN ARRANGEMENT SUCH
AS THIS, WITH THREE FLOWERS, THERE
ARE ONLY TWO DIFFERENT TECHNIQUES.

PATTERNS

Beaded flower patterns are written
in a type of shorthand, not unlike
knitting patterns, in which abbreviations indicate specific beading
instructions.

A pattern tells you what techniques
you'll use and how many repetitions
of them you need. It also tells you
the amount of beads you'll need,
indicated in one of two ways: either
as a specific number of beads or in
the number of inches of beaded
wire. (This will be more clear as
you work through the steps in this

chapter and refer when indicated
to the Flower-Making Math section
on the opposite page.)

It's easy to learn to read the
patterns because there are only
four basic patterns—for the four
basic techniques and the two
shapes—round or pointed—that
the tops and bottoms of the petals
and leaves can have. That's a total
of only eight abbreviations you
need to know to make all of the
flowers in this book.

BEADED FLOWER PATTERN ABBREVIATIONS

BF . . . . .Basic Frame
CL . . . . .Continuous Loops
CCL . . . .Continuous
          Crossover Loops
CWL . . . .Continuous
          Wraparound Loops
PB . . . . .Pointed Bottom
PT . . . . .Pointed Top
RB . . . . .Round Bottom
RT . . . . .Round Top

THE MATH IN FLOWER-MAKING IS EASY. YOU'LL LEARN ITS BASICS WHEN YOU MAKE THE POPPY, STARTING ON PAGE 33.

Estimating the *exact* number of beads to put on the wire can be tricky when you're new to beading flowers, but you'll quickly get the knack for it. It's a straightforward process of reading the pattern, doing some simple math, and having a little experience. Here are some tips and a few sample formulas that you can apply to any pattern in the book.

1 The CL pattern for the inner center of the poppy (page 33) is an example of a super-easy pattern. It says "Make 3 7-bead loops." How many beads do you need? Answer: 3 loops x 7 beads =21 total beads needed.

If the pattern says, "Make 3 1-inch loops," it's still easy. You'll need 3 inches of beads on the wire for sure, but go ahead and add 1 extra inch, just in case your loops were a little bigger.

2 In a CCL pattern, you have a set of 2 loops. The second loop will always be a little bigger than the first, usually about ½ inch bigger. The poppy calyx pattern (page 34) says, "Make 5 CCL beginning with a 1-½-inch loop of beads." Since the crossover (or second) loop will be about 2 inches of beads, that's roughly 3½ inches for each set of crossover loops. How many inches of beads do you need to make the whole patttern? Answer: 5 sets of crossover loops x 3½ inches = 18 inches of beads + 2 extra inches for safety =
20 total inches of beads needed.

3 In a CWL pattern, you can have an unlimited number of loop sets. The loops will increase in size as you add them. I usually allow a 50 percent increase for each additional wraparound loop.

The pattern for the outer center of the poppy (page 35) says, "Make 5 CWL, 2 loops each, beginning with a 1-inch bead loop." How many inches of beads will you need? Answer: 1-inch loop of beads to begin with + 1 wraparound loop = 2½ inches of beads for each set x 5 sets = 13 inches of beads + 2 inches extra for safety = 15 total inches of beads needed.

4 In a BF pattern, you wrap a specified number of rows of beads around a basic row of beads, so you'd estimate the number of beads in the basic row in inches. If you're using size 11/0 beads, 1 inch of beaded wire would hold about 20 beads. Each subsequent row in the pattern will get longer and require more beads—in my formula, I usually triple the number of beads in the basic row and multiply that by the total number of rows.

The pattern for the poppy leaf on page 36 says, "20-bead BF...9 rows." How many inches of beads will you need? Answer: 1 inch (20 beads) x 3 = 3 inches in basic row x 9 rows = 27 inches + 3 inches for safety = 30 total inches of beads needed.

TIP: If you run out of beads on the wire, you can always add more. Simply estimate the amount of bare wire that you'll need to complete the flower part. Add about 8 inches of bare wire so that you will have enough wire to hold in your hand and clip the bare wire from the spool. Add the beads onto the end of the wire, knot it to keep the beads from falling off, and continue working.

TIP: If you add too many beads to the wire, you can always remove them.

TIP: For measurements in metrics, see the metric conversion chart at the back of the book on page 128.

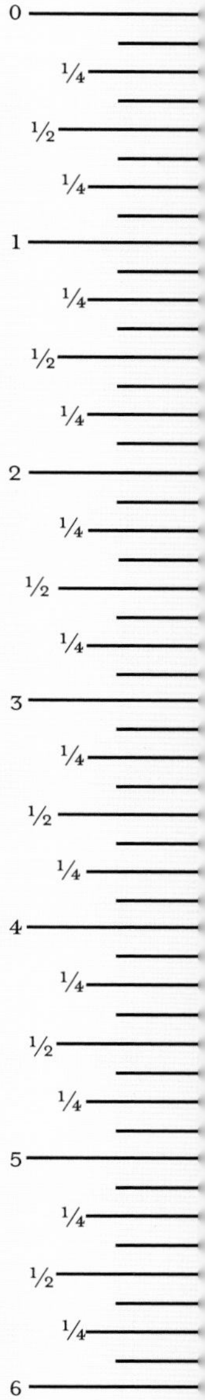

0
¼
½
¼
1
¼
½
¼
2
¼
½
¼
3
¼
½
¼
4
¼
½
¼
5
¼
½
¼
6

Basic Technique #1: Continuous Loops (CL)

A *simple loop* is a section of wire with a *specific number of beads* strung on it with bare wire at both ends. The bare ends are twisted together, forming a loop of beads. All three of the basic loop techniques use the simple loop as their essential element.

Simple loops can be made in succession, resulting in *a strip of loops side by side on a single wire*. These are *Continuous Loops (CL)*. This technique is used for leaves, calyxes, and centers. The Continuous Loops are the simplest of the four techniques and produce a light and airy effect.

Tip: When making loops, always twist the loops in the same direction to keep the beads from falling off.

Tip: When making a flower part with one of the loop techniques, some beaders hold the loop and twist it to secure it; others wrap the wire around the loop. Do what is most comfortable for you.

THE CLOVER USES A STRIP OF
27 CONTINUOUS LOOPS (CLs)
FOR ITS PETALS.

Basic Technique #2: Continuous Crossover Loops (CCL)

A *crossover loop* is a *simple loop with another loop of beaded wire wrapped around it in a specific way:* from the bottom of the first loop, over its top, and then back to its bottom. Like continuous loops, crossover loops can be made in succession on a single wire to create a strip. These are *Continuous Crossover Loops (CCL)*. They look like 4 rows of beads clustered together and are frequently used to make petals and calyxes.

Basic Technique #3: Continuous Wraparound Loops (CWL)

A *wraparound loop* is a *simple loop with at least 1 loop of beaded wire wrapped around it*. The wraparound loop doesn't touch the simple loop, but circles it along its outside. Like continuous loops and continuous crossover loops, you can make a series of wraparound loops in succession on a single wire. These are *Continuous Wraparound Loops (CWL)*.

The pattern for CWLs will tell you how many sets of loops you'll need on the strip, how many total loops will be in each set, and how many beads are required—stated either as the *exact number of beads* or the *number of inches*.

THE VIOLET USES CONTINUOUS
CROSSOVER LOOPS (CCLs) FOR PETALS.

THE PEONY HAS AS MANY AS
8 CONTINUOUS WRAPAROUND LOOPS
(CWLs) IN ITS PETAL SECTIONS.

Basic Technique #4: Basic Frame (BF)

The *basic frame* technique is based on bending the beaded wire to create *a frame that holds a basic row of beads*—thus its name, the basic frame. Think of the basic row as the center vein of a leaf, around which you wrap rows of beaded wire a specified number of times.

The frame has a top and a bottom. When you twist the wire around the basic row at a *45° angle*, you'll make a *pointed top (PT)* or *pointed bottom (PB)*. When you twist the wire around the basic row at a *90° angle*, you get a *round top (RT)* or *round bottom (RB)*.

PARTS OF THE BASIC FRAME

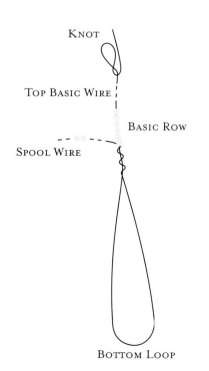

Knot

Top Basic Wire

Basic Row

Spool Wire

Bottom Loop

EACH PETAL HAS A FRONT (LEFT) AND A BACK (RIGHT). THE BACKSIDE OF THE PETAL WILL SHOW WHERE YOU TWISTED THE WIRE. THE TWISTED WIRES SHOULD APPEAR IN A STRAIGHT LINE. IF THEY AREN'T IN A STRAIGHT LINE, HOLD THE FRAME STRAIGHTER.

THE DAFFODIL PETAL USES THE BASIC (BF) TECHNIQUE WITH A POINTED TOP (PT) AND A POINTED BOTTOM (PB).

THE INNER GARDENIA PETAL USES THE BASIC FRAME (BF) TECHNIQUE WITH A ROUND TOP (RT) AND A POINTED BOTTOM (PB).

It may seem complicated at first, and I have to admit it's a challenge to learn, but the basic frame technique is so versatile you'll use it more than any other. Merely by changing the pattern—just a little bit—you can create a myriad of petals and leaves—with ends that are pointed or round, narrow or wide, long or short, or any desired combination.

The number of beads or the number of inches of beads that you start with in the basic row determines the length of the leaf or petal—the more beads you use in this row, the longer the leaf or petal will be. The number of times that you twist the beaded wire around the basic row determines how wide the leaf or petal will be. It's that simple!

TIP: To create a tight-looking petal, keep the rows as close together as you can. With your fingers, mold the petal as you make the rows.

TIP: When wrapping wire around the basic row, some beaders twist the petal and others twist the wire. Do whatever feels most natural for you.

REDUCING WIRES TO MAKE STEMS

When a pattern for the basic frame says reduce to 1, 2, or 3 wires, it means to create a stem with the available wires (the spool wire and the bottom loop wire). (See figure 1.) For small petals or leaves you'd normally reduce to 1 wire as you did in step 2 in Making the Poppy Leaf. Reducing to 2 or 3 wires makes a sturdier stem. (See figure 2.)

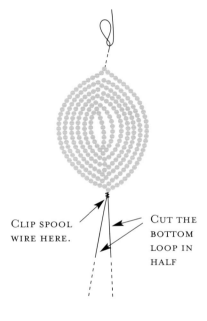

CLIP SPOOL WIRE HERE.

CUT THE BOTTOM LOOP IN HALF

FIGURE 1. WHEN THE PATTERN SAYS REDUCE TO 2 WIRES HERE'S WHAT YOU DO. FIRST, CLIP OFF THE BARE SPOOL WIRE AT THE BASE OF THE PETAL OR LEAF, CUTTING IT CLOSE, WITHOUT LEAVING A TAIL. SECONDLY, CUT THE BOTTOM LOOP IN HALF, RESULTING IN 2 WIRES—TWIST THOSE WIRES TOGETHER TO MAKE 1 TWISTED WIRE, WHICH IS THE STEM.

LEAVE A 2-INCH TAIL OF SPOOL WIRE.

CUT THE BOTTOM LOOP IN HALF.

FIGURE 2. TO REDUCE TO 3 WIRES, CLIP OFF THE BARE SPOOL WIRE, LEAVING A TAIL OF 2 TO 3 INCHES. CUT THE BOTTOM LOOP IN HALF, RESULTING IN 2 WIRES— JOIN THEM WITH THE TAIL WIRE AND TWIST ALL 3 TOGETHER TO MAKE 1 TWISTED WIRE.

Uh Oh!

"MY LOOPS KEEP COMING UNDONE!"

Remember to twist the loops in the same direction.

"MY LEAVES ARE ROUND AT THE TOP AND THEY'RE SUPPOSED TO BE POINTED."

You're not holding the wire at a 45° angle. Don't be afraid to leave a little bare wire at the top. It will get covered up.

"I DON'T HAVE ENOUGH SPACE TO WRAP THE ROWS FOR THE BASIC FRAME."

Leave a longer top basic wire.

"I CAN'T TELL WHICH IS THE FRONT OF THE PETAL AND WHICH IS THE BACK. I HAVE WIRES ON BOTH SIDES."

Always work from the front of the petal. Unless the instructions say something else, always wrap the wire in front of the top basic wire and in front of the bottom loop.

"I DIDN'T PUT ENOUGH BEADS ON THE WIRE AND I'M ONLY HALFWAY THROUGH THE LEAF."

It's not the end of the world. Estimate how much wire you need to complete the leaf, add about 8 inches and clip from the spool. String beads onto the bare wire, knot it and get back to work!

"MY STEM IS TOO THICK."

The key to a good-looking stem is to be neat with the assembly. Taper the wires of the petals and leaves so that the stem is thicker at the top than it is on the bottom.

"MY STEM IS LUMPY."

Keep assembly wire as smooth as possible around the stem. Also, don't take the thicker wires such as petal, leaf or calyx wires and wrap around the stem. Use assembly wire to secure these to the stem.

"MY FLOWER LOOKS LIKE IT'S WILTING!"

The key to successful and sound assembly is to add each petal or component part one at a time. Hold the base of the petal as close to the stem as you can wrap two or three times with assembly wire. Pull the wire straight and add the next petal in the same way.

BASIC TECHNIQUES ARE INDICATED FOR EACH PROJECT, SUCH AS CONTINUOUS LOOPS AND BASIC FRAME FOR THE POINSETTIA.

SPECIAL TECHNIQUES, SUCH AS STRIPING, ARE LISTED IN THE PROJECT WITH REFERENCE TO ANOTHER PROJECT WHERE THE TECHNIQUE IS DESCRIBED IN DETAIL.

NEW TECHNIQUES, SUCH AS BEADING THE STEM, ARE DETAILED IN ONE PROJECT AND REFERENCED IN OTHER PROJECTS.

ABOUT THE PROJECT INSTRUCTIONS

There are 21 projects in *The Art of French Beaded Flowers,* totaling 30 blooms, plus a variety of foliage, and a few very handsome bugs. The project instructions are organized in such a way to help you easily select a project, gather needed materials, and then make and assemble the completed flower. Here are the sections you'll find in each set of instructions.

THREE CATEGORIES OF TECHNIQUES

There are three categories of techniques that can be used in any one project. They are listed at the beginning of the project instructions, so you'll know what techniques will be required before you begin.

Basic Techniques include one or more of the four fundamental construction methods needed for every project. These techniques are expressed in patterns.

Special Techniques are often-used additional techniques which will be needed in the particular project.

New Techniques are special methods that are introduced in that project and explained in detail.

PARTS OF THE FLOWER

This is a thumbnail sketch of how simple or complex the project might be, depending on how many parts are in the flower.

WHAT YOU NEED

This is the list of the materials and supplies you need to complete (usually, but not always) one flower. Just multiply the amounts listed to arrive at what you'd need to make

multiple flowers. You'll notice that the lists always end with the Basic Flower-Making Kit described on page 18.

STEP-BY-STEP INSTRUCTIONS FOR CONSTRUCTION & ASSEMBLY

Project instructions are divided into two categories: how to make the parts of the flower, and how to assemble them. The *construction* steps generally start with the petals, which take the largest number of beads, and then continue with the leaves and the other parts.

The *assembly* instructions specify how to create a stem, either by twisting wires, or adding stiff stem wires. The order of assembly is usually the same: stamens are usually added first, followed by any other part in the center, then petals, sepals, or calyx, and finally the leaves. Some flowers require a unique assembly, which is covered in detail in the specific project.

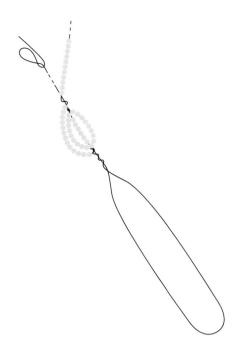

FIGURE 3. ILLUSTRATIONS CLARIFY BEAD PLACEMENT. THIS IS WHAT THE BEADS AND WIRES WOULD REALLY LOOK LIKE, WITH A LONG LOOP AND LONG SPOOL WIRE.

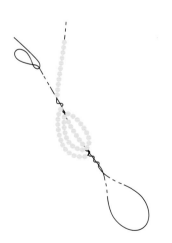

FIGURE 4. TO SAVE SPACE, THE ILLUSTRATIONS CUT SHORT THE LENGTH OF THE WIRES, INDICATED BY DASHED LINES.

HOW TO USE THIS BOOK

As you start making projects from this book, you'll probably find yourself frequently flipping back and forth among the pages of the book, especially to this chapter and the first project, the Classic Poppy Pin on page 33. You'll also be cross-referencing among projects for instructions on special techniques that are detailed in only one project but used in many. Until it becomes second nature to estimate how many beads you'll need, go ahead and make a copy of the section on flower-making math on page 25, so you can have it nearby while you work. Remember to use the handy ruler on the same page to help you measure and cut your beaded wire.

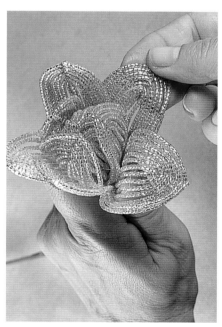

THE HOW-TO PHOTOS SHOW HAND PLACEMENT TIPS—HOW TO HOLD, MOLD, AND BEND THE WIRES AND THE FLOWER PARTS AS YOU ARE MAKING AND ASSEMBLING THEM.

YOU'LL NEVER RUN OUT OF OCCASIONS TO CELEBRATE WITH FRENCH BEADED FLOWERS.

If you find yourself wanting to change patterns and write your own tips on the pages so you can share what you learned with others, go right ahead—I couldn't be more pleased.

When you first make beaded flowers, you may feel like you're all thumbs. Congratulations—you're normal! Just as in any other craft, your beaded flower-making skills will improve with time. Your second flower will certainly look better than your first, and after you've made a few bouquets, you'll look at the prospect of a new project with a changed perspective. A vase with only three flowers? "I'll make a dozen!" An ordinary daffodil with one color? "Not for me—I'll give it five colors, including gold and silver and a beaded butterfly or two." Enjoy!

The bright red poppy symbolizes different things to different people. As the favored flower of the goddess Demeter, it's a token of nature's fertility. For military veterans it's a badge of honor. With its five petals and two centers, the poppy has become the classic sampler for beaded flowermakers. By following its detailed instructions and completing it, you'll learn the four basic techniques used in all the other projects in the book.

Basic Techniques

Continuous Loops
Continuous Crossover Loops
Continuous Wraparound Loops
Basic Frame

Poppy

5 petals
1 leaf
1 inner center
1 outer center
1 calyx

Classic Poppy Pin

What You Need for 1 Poppy

1 hank	11/0 red beads for petals
1 hank	11/0 green beads for leaf and calyx
1 strand	11/0 yellow beads for inner center
1 strand	11/0 black beads for outer center
1 spool	26-gauge red wire for petals
1 spool	26-gauge green wire for leaf and calyx
1 spool	26-gauge gold wire for inner center
1 spool	26-gauge black wire for outer center
1 spool	30 to 34-gauge assembly wire
1 pin back (found in craft or bead stores)
Basic Flower-Making Kit (see page 18)

Making the Inner Center of the Poppy

PATTERN

Make 3 CL with 7 beads each. Leave 3 inches of bare wire on each side.

WHAT IT MEANS

Make 3 continuous loops (3 CL) on 1 wire, each with 7 beads.

WHAT YOU DO

1 String a wire with 21 beads. (Why 21 beads? See step 1 in Flower-Making Math on page 25).

2 Make sure that the wire is knotted at its loose end so the beads don't fall off.

3 Push 7 beads up to within 3 inches of the knot. Make a loop. Twist the wire at the bottom of the loop 1 complete turn.

To make the poppy larger, simply add more rows to the petals and leaf.

Photo 1. You've made 2 loops and are ready to start the 3rd.

4 Leave ⅛ inch of bare wire and make another 7-bead loop. Unless the pattern specifies otherwise, ⅛ inch is the standard distance between continuous loops. (See photo 1.)

5 Repeat step 4 and you will have 3 CLs.

6 After you finish the last loop, wrap the wire around the loop 1 more time to secure it.

7 As the pattern indicates, leave 3 inches of bare wire after the last loop and clip the wire from the spool. You've finished the first part of your first flower.

MAKING THE CALYX FOR THE POPPY

PATTERN

Make 5 CCL beginning with a 1½-inch loop of beads. Leave 2 inches of bare wire at either end.

WHAT IT MEANS

Make 5 continuous crossover loops on 1 wire, and each one will begin with a 1½-inch loop of beads. You'll have 2 inches of bare wire on each side of the strip of loops.

PHOTO 2. YOU'VE COMPLETED 1 CCL AND ARE READY FOR THE NEXT ONE.

WHAT YOU DO

1 String about 18 inches of beads on the spool of wire. (Why 18 inches? See step 2 in Flower-Making Math on 25.)

2 Make sure that the loose end of the wire is knotted so the beads don't fall off.

3 Push 1½ inches of beads up to within 2 inches of the knot and make a simple loop. Twist the wire at the bottom of the loop 1 complete turn. The beaded wire is at the bottom of the loop. Bring it up over the top of the simple loop, press it between 2 beads at the top of the loop, and bring it down the other side. Hold the beads in place and twist the loop 1 complete turn to secure the loop and the beads. (See photo 2.)

4 You'll need more space between these loops than the continuous loops. Leave ¼ inch of bare wire and repeat step 3. Continue making loops with ¼ inch of bare wire after each loop until you have the required 5CCLs

5 After you finish the last loop, wrap the wire around the loop 1 more time to secure it.

6 Leave about 2 inches of wire and clip from the spool. Remember to knot the wire on the spool.

MAKING THE OUTER CENTER OF THE POPPY

PATTERN

Make 5 CWL, 2 loops each, beginning with a 1-inch bead loop. Leave 2 inches of bare wire on each side.

WHAT IT MEANS

Make 5 sets of loops on a single wire. Each set will have 1 loop and another slightly larger loop wrapped around it. You'll have 1½ inches of bare wire on either side of the loops.

WHAT YOU DO

1 String about 15 inches of beads on the spool of wire. (Why 15 inches? See step 3 in Flower-Making Math on page 25.)

2 Make sure that the loose end of the wire is knotted so the beads don't fall off.

3 Push 1 inch of beads up to within 2 inches of the knot, make a simple loop, and twist the loop 1 complete turn. Move the beaded wire to the left side of this

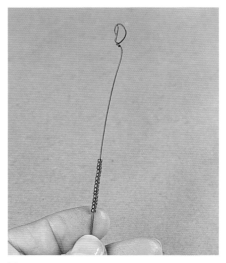

PHOTO 3. YOU'VE COMPLETED 2 CONTINUOUS WRAPAROUND LOOPS AND ARE READY FOR THE 3RD.

PHOTO 4. THIS IS THE BASIC ROW FOR THE POPPY LEAF.

loop, and then wrap it completely around the outside so you make another loop, bigger than the 1st one. Hold the beads in place, and twist both loops 1 complete turn to secure them.

4 Leave ¼ inch of bare wire and repeat step 3. Continue making loops with ¼ inch of bare wire after each loop until you have the required 5 CWL. (See photo 3.) Note: If you're adding more than 1 wraparound loop, you'll need more bare wire in between the loops.

5 After you finish the last set of loops, wrap the wire around them 1 more time to secure them.

6 Leave about 2 inches of bare wire and clip from the spool. Remember to knot the wire on the spool.

MAKING THE POPPY LEAF

For most beaded flower projects, you'll make the petal first. The poppy is the exception. For purposes of learning the Basic Frame technique, you'll make the leaf first. Having a pointed top (PT) and a round bottom (RB), the leaf is slightly more complicated than the petal, whose top and bottom are both round.

PATTERN

20-bead BF, PT, RB, 9 rows, reduce to 1 wire.

WHAT IT MEANS

Make a leaf with a pointed top (PT) and a round bottom (RB) with 9 rows across. You'll start with a basic row with 20 beads. When the leaf is completed, you'll cut open the loop to "reduce" it to just 1 wire for the stem.

WHAT YOU DO

1 String about 30 inches of beads on the spool of wire. (Why 30 inches? See step 4 in Flower-Making Math on page 25.) Make sure that the wire is knotted at its loose end so the beads don't fall off.

2 Make the basic row, which is Row 1. Push 1 inch of beads up to within 2 inches of the knot. This basic row will be the center row of your leaf. The knotted end is the top of the basic row. With your right hand and fingers, hold the beads in place on the basic row. Be sure to leave 2 inches of bare wire at the top of the beads because you'll need it to work the next steps. (See photo 4.)

3 With your left hand and 6 inches of the bare wire that is attached to the spool, make a 3-inch loop. Put the ends of the loop together in your right hand. (See photo 5.) Place 3 or 4 fingers of your left hand in the loop, and use your

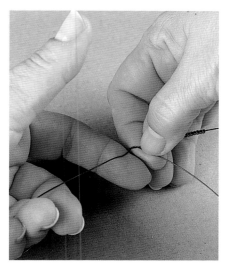

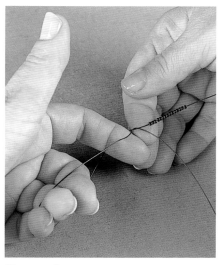

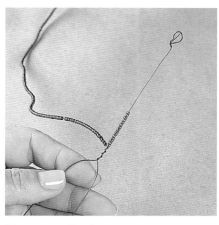

PHOTO 5. WITH 6 INCHES OF WIRE, MAKE A 3-INCH LOOP.

PHOTO 6. WITH YOUR FINGERS IN THE LOOP, TWIST THE WIRES TIGHTLY ABOUT 5 TIMES.

PHOTO 7. YOU'VE COMPLETED THE BASIC FRAME FOR THE LEAF.

fingers to make a twist at the bottom end of the basic row. Twist tightly about 5 times. You've completed the basic frame! (See photo 6.)

4 Hold the basic frame upright (the loop will be at the bottom) and wrap the beaded wire around the twist until it's on the left side of the basic row. You're ready to begin Row 2. (See photo 7.)

5 Complete Row 2. Bring the beaded wire up the left side of the frame and hold it close to the basic row. Push the beads down the wire flush against the twist. The pattern calls for a pointed top (PT). Hold the top of the beaded wire in front of and at a 45° angle above the basic row of beads. Wrap the bare wire completely around the top basic wire, maintaining the 45° angle. You've completed row 2. (See photo 8.)

6 Prepare the frame to put on the next row. Bend the beaded wire down close to the basic row. With

the front of the leaf facing you, rotate the frame 180° counter-clockwise so that the loop is pointing up away from you. The top of the leaf with the knot is now pointed down and the bottom of the leaf with the twisted loop is pointed up. You're ready to start Row 3.

7 Complete Row 3. Bring the beaded wire up the left side again. The pattern calls for a round bottom (RB), which means you'll hold the bare wire in front of bottom loop and straight across at a 90° angle. Twist the bare wire completely around the twisted loop. (See photo 9.)

8 Prepare the frame for row 4 and complete it. With the front of the leaf facing you, rotate the frame 180° counter-clockwise so that the loop is pointing down again and the top basic wire is pointing up. Bring the beaded wire around to the left side and up to the top basic. Hold the wire at a 45° angle and twist. You've completed Row 4.

PHOTO 8. YOU'VE COMPLETED ROW 2 OF THE LEAF.

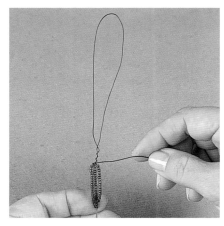

PHOTO 9. YOU'VE COMPLETED ROW 3 OF THE LEAF.

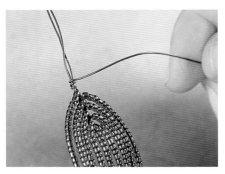

PHOTO 11. TWIST BARE WIRE AROUND THE LOOP 2 TIMES TO SECURE IT.

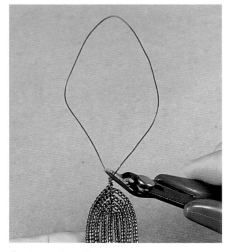

PHOTO 12. CLIP 1 SIDE OF THE BASIC LOOP TO REDUCE THE WIRES TO 1 AND MAKE THE STEM.

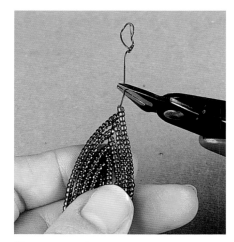

PHOTO 13. CLIP THE TOP BASIC WIRE TO ⅛ INCH AND BEND TO THE BACK.

PHOTO 10. YOU'VE COMPLETED ROW 9.

9 Continue to add 5 more rows until you have a total of 9 rows, 4 rows on either side of the basic row. (See photo 10.) After you add each row, with the front of the leaf facing you, turn the frame 180° counter-clockwise. Bring the beaded wire to the left side to make the next row. At the loop, hold the wire at a 90° angle to make a round bottom; at the top basic, hold the wire at a 45° angle to make a pointed top.

10 When you have completed row 9, you've finished the leaf. You'll be at the base of the leaf. Wrap the bare wire around the twist 2 more times to secure it. (See photo 11.)

11 Clip off the beaded spool wire, leaving still attached the bottom loop of the basic frame.

12 Reduce the loop to 1 wire to make the stem. Cut 1 end of the loop at the base of the leaf, resulting in 1 long wire, which is now the stem of the leaf. (See photo 12.)

13 Clip the top basic wire to ⅜ inch and bend it to the back side of the leaf to hide it. You can use your fingers or a pair of pliers. You've finished the leaf! Now you're ready to make the petal. (See photo 13.)

MAKING THE POPPY PETAL

PATTERN

Make 5, 8-bead BF, RT, RB, 11 rows, reduce to 1 wire.

WHAT IT MEANS

Make 5 petals with a round top and round bottom with 11 rows across, and reduce it to 1 wire.

WHAT YOU DO

Start with an 8-bead basic row. Proceed exactly as you did with the leaf, with one exception. The petal pattern calls for a rounded top and a rounded bottom. Thus, after you make the basic frame, you'll wrap the rows holding the beaded wire at a 90° angle at both ends of the basic row.

PHOTO 14. PLACE THE YELLOW INNER CENTER IN THE MIDDLE OF THE BLACK OUTER CENTER.

PHOTO 15. ADD EACH PETAL, ONE AT A TIME.

PHOTO 16. USE ASSEMBLY WIRE TO SECURE THE CALYX.

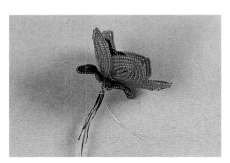

PHOTO 17. WRAP ASSEMBLY WIRE DOWN THE STEM ABOUT 3 INCHES.

PHOTO 18. WRAP THE STEM WITH FLORAL TAPE.

ASSEMBLING THE POPPY

1 Make 1 completed center by placing the yellow inner center in the middle of the black outer center. Form the stem by carefully twisting the wires together tightly with the nylon jaw-nose or flat-nose pliers. (See photo 14.)

2 Hold 1 petal under the completed center so that its bottom is snug against the base of the center. (See photo 15.) At the point where they meet, wrap assembly wire around them about 3 times, making sure the petal is securely fastened. In the same manner, add each of the remaining 4 petals, 1 at a time, distributing them evenly around the stem.

3 Place the calyx under the petals and around the stem. Pull the wires around the stem to evenly distribute the calyx's sepals. (See photo 16.)

4 From the base of the flower to about 3 inches down the stem, wrap all the wires tightly with assembly wire. (See photo 17.)

5 With wire cutters, cut the wires so the stem is natural looking— thicker at the top and thinner at bottom. Clip the assembly wire from the spool.

6 Cut an 8-inch piece of floral tape on the diagonal and stretch the top of it to make it sticky. Press the tip of the tape around the base of the petals with one hand, taking care to cover any wire. Then use your other hand to wrap the tape around the stem, on a diagonal like a peppermint candy cane, pulling as you go. (See photo 18.)

7 About ½ inch below the base of the petals, hold the base of the leaf to the stem and wrap them together with the floral tape. Continue wrapping the stem with the floral tape on a diagonal, stretching and pulling tightly as you go until you reach the end of the stem wire.

8 Bend each of the 5 points of the calyx down and shape the petals of the flower so they cup inward.

9 Cut the stem to about 2 inches below the base of the flower. Wrap the pin back onto the stem with floral tape.

PHOTO 19. WRAP THE LEAF BASE TO THE STEM.

PHOTO 20. WRAP THE PIN BACK TO THE STEM.

USE THE POPPY PIN'S ASSEMBLY TECHNIQUES WITH ANY FLOWER TO MAKE LAPEL PINS, CORSAGES, AND DECORATIONS FOR HATS AND HANDBAGS.

Glass House Dahlia

The Aztecs were the first to fall in love with the glorious multi-petaled dahlia. Today its easy-to-grow nature makes it popular in gardens all over the world. With petals in two sun-dazzled colors, some with shaded tips, the dahlia becomes a jewel glimmering in its own glass house.

Basic Technique

Basic Frame (BF)

Special Techniques

Beading the Stem
Tipping the Edges

Dahlia

47 petals of 6 different sizes
1 small leaf (with 7 leaflets)
1 large leaf (with 7 leaflets)
1 calyx

PETALS TIPPED WITH ANOTHER COLOR
ARE VIBRANT AND EXTRA SPARKLY.

WHAT YOU NEED
FOR 1 DAHLIA

2 hanks	11/0 (color A) beads for petals (any color you like, I used yellow)
1 hank	11/0 (color B) beads for petals (any color you like, I used orange)
1 hank	11/0 green seed or bugle beads for leaves
1 spool	24-gauge gold wire for petals
1 spool	24-gauge green wire for leaves

Basic Flower-Making Kit

MAKING THE PARTS
OF THE DAHLIA

1 Make 5 very small color B petals. Pattern: 4-bead BF, RT, RB, 5 rows, reduce to 1 wire.

2 Make 5 small color A petals, and tip the edges with color B beads. Pattern: 6-bead BF, RT, RB, 5 rows, reduce to 1 wire. (See the instructions on tipping the edges in the Holiday Wreath Centerpiece project on page 115. You'll tip the edges of petals in this step and in steps, 3, and 4.)

3 Make 5 medium color A petals, and tip the edges with color B beads. Pattern: 9-bead BF, RT, RB, 5 rows, reduce to 1 wire. Tip the end of each petal with color B beads.

4 Make 10 large color A petals, tipping 5 of them with color B beads. Pattern: 12-bead BF, RT, RB, 5 rows, reduce to 1 wire.

5 Make 10 extra-large color A petals. Pattern: 14-bead BF, RT, RB, 5 rows, reduce to 1 wire.

6 Make 12 extra-extra-large color A petals. Pattern: 14-bead BF, RT, RB, 7 rows, reduce to 1 wire.

7 The dahlia leaves, both small and large, are the same as the leaves in the Party Perfect Peony project. See Making the Parts of the Peony, steps 3 and 4, on pages 72 and 73.

8 Make the calyx with seed beads (or bugle beads, if you wish). Pattern: Make 5 CWL, 3 loops each, beginning with a 1½-inch loop. Before adding the 2nd and

3rd loops, squeeze the 1st loop to form a point. As you wrap the 2nd and 3rd loops, create a point at the top. Leave 3 inches of bare wire on each side.

ASSEMBLING THE DAHLIA

1 Take 2 of the smallest petals and, with the wire sides facing each other, use nylon jaw-nose or flat-nose pliers to twist together the wires. This will become the stem for the flower.

2 Beginning with the 3 remaining smallest petals, add all the petals to the stem, increasing in size as you go. Attach them at right angles, with the wire side facing down, twisting the wires carefully with the pliers. When you add the large petals (that you made in step 4 at left), alternate between the tipped petals and the single color petals.

3 Add the calyx.

4 Bead the stem (see the instructions in the Three Cheery Spring Bulbs project on page 49) and add the leaves about 1 and 2 inches below the base of the blossom.

DESIGN TIP

Take the dahlia out of the house and sew it on to a handbag or sturdy tote—you'll be amazed at the number of curious strangers who stop to admire your stunning creation!

Tussie Mussie with Red Clover

*B*ring back bygone days with tiny wildflowers in a pretty tussie-mussie. The clover blossoms are easily made with continuous loops; the trifoliate leaves are simple basic frames.

Basic Techniques

Basic Frame (BF)
Continuous Loops (CL)

Clover

1 blossom
6 leaves

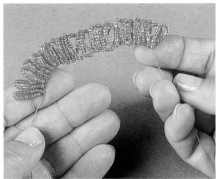

PHOTO 1. MAKE THE CLOVER BLOSSOM.

PHOTO 2. START THE ASSEMBLY OF
THE CLOVER.

WHAT YOU NEED FOR
1 RED CLOVER

1 hank	11/0 or 12/0 reddish pink beads for blossom
1 hank	11/0 green beads for leaves
1 spool	26-gauge colored wire for blossoms
1 spool	24-gauge green wire for leaves
1 piece	18-gauge stem wire, cut to 8 inches, and wrapped with floral tape

Basic Flower-Making Kit

MAKING THE PARTS OF
THE RED CLOVER

1   Make the blossom. Pattern: Make 27 CL with 1 inch of beads each. Leave 3 inches of bare wire on either end. After you make the 27 loops, gently twist each loop. (See photo 1.)

2   Make 6 leaves. Pattern: 4-bead BF, PT, PB, 5 rows, reduce to 1 wire.

ASSEMBLING THE
RED CLOVER

1   Hold 1 end of the 27-loop strip and roll the loops clockwise around the first loop about 4 times or until you get to the end. As you twist, you'll add a layer of loops slightly below the previous one. (See photo 2.)

2   When you have reached the end of the loops, tightly twist together the 2 wires (the beginning and the ending wires). Attach the blossom to the stem.

3   Add the leaves in groups of 3, one set directly under the blossom and the other along the stem.

4   Repeat all the above steps to make as many flowers as you wish. I used 5 clovers for the bouquet in the photo.

5   You may have to trim the stems to make a small arrangement fit into a tussie mussie holder. Use floral clay to keep the flowers secure

DESIGN TIP

Clover is a wonderful filler flower in arrangements and bouquets. It's absolutely lovely in the Beaded Bridal Bouquet on page 93.

Floating Gardenia

The delicate gardenia needs nothing more than a simple pottery bowl to show off its serene beauty. You'll construct its petals with thin 28-gauge wire, making them flexible enough to be shaped into gentle curves. Don't worry about the wires showing when you turn back the petals—with the reverse basic technique you can choose to hide the wires on their tops or bottoms.

Basic Technique

Basic Frame (BF)

Special Technique

Lacing

New Technique

Reverse Basic

Gardenia

17 petals (3 small, 5 medium, 9 large)
5 leaves

MAKING THE PARTS
OF THE GARDENIA

1 Make 3 small petals. Pattern: 7-bead BF, RT, PB, 11 rows, reduce to 1 wire.

2 See reverse basic instructions on the bottom of page 47 opposite. Make 5 medium petals. Pattern: 8-bead BF, RT, PB, reverse basic 11 rows, reduce to 1 wire.

3 Make 9 large petals. Pattern: 11-bead BF, RT, PB, 13 rows, reduce to 1 wire.

4 Make 5 leaves. Pattern: 18-bead BF, RT, PB, 17 rows, reduce to 3 wires and twist them together. See lacing instructions in the Three Cheery Spring Bulbs project on page 49 and lace each leaf, catching at least every 3rd row.

ASSEMBLING THE GARDENIA

1 Cup the 3 small and 5 medium petals by gently pushing your thumb into the bottom petal (thumb to wire side).

2 With the wire side facing in, hold the 3 small petals so they are facing each other. Twist the wires together to form the stem.

3 Add the 5 medium petals around the small ones with the bottom wire against the small petals. With your fingers, curl the petal tops slightly to the back. Notice how the wires at the top are hidden.

WHAT YOU NEED
FOR 1 GARDENIA

3 hanks	12/0 white beads for petals
3 hanks	11/0 green beads for leaves
1 spool	28-gauge white wire for petals
1 spool	24-gauge green wire for leaves
1 spool	30 to 34-gauge green lacing wire for leaf base
1 spool	30 to 34-gauge white assembly wire for petals

Shallow bowl with opening large enough to hold the gardenia
Floral clay (optional)
Basic Flower-Making Kit

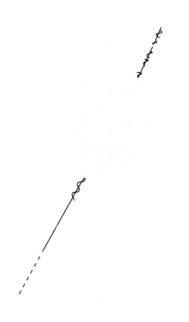

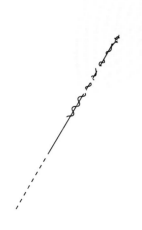

4 Add the 9 outer petals at right angles to the blossom.

5 Twist all the wires and cover with floral tape.

6 With lacing wire, make the leaf base by weaving the 5 petals together, catching at least every 3rd row with the wire. Connect the leaves to make a circle. Leave a small opening in the center.

7 Place the stem of the gardenia blossom in the leaf base. Wrap with floral tape.

8 Trim the stem to a suitable length for your bowl. If necessary, use floral clay at the bottom of the bowl to secure the stem.

NEW TECHNIQUE

REVERSE BASIC

Usually when you make a leaf or a petal, it has a full front side, where little if any wire shows, and a full back side, which shows wire. For some flowers, such as the gardenia and certain roses, you'll want to curl the top of a petal over, revealing its back side, but you don't want the backside wire to show. The reverse basic is a technique that allows you hide the wire on the side that you see.

When you make the petal, instead of bringing the wire in front of the bottom loop, bring it around the back side, and then make the twist. When you're finished, you'll have a petal with wire on one side at the top and on the other side at the bottom. (See figures at left.)

Lavender Camellia

Once you learn how to make a gardenia, you can easily make a camellia. It's smaller and comes in different colors than the gardenia, but the construction techniques are similar.

To make the camellia, follow the same pattern as the gardenia with a few changes. Use 5 lavender beads for the basic row. Reduce the number of rows in the petals this way: to 7 for the small petals, to 9 for the medium ones, and to 11 for the large petals.

To make a hair accessory, use assembly wire to attach the completed flower to a barrette or comb.

Celebrate spring cheer all year with this joyful trio that displays several techniques in one arrangement. The daffodil with its pointed petals has a center trumpet made out of continuous loops laced together. The iris beard peeks out between two petals with both rounded and pointed ends. The tulip has petals that bend both inward and outward around a group of stamens. They all have a long-stemmed glow thanks to their beaded stems.

Basic Techniques

Continuous Loops (CL)
Basic Frame (BF)

Special Techniques

Reverse Basic

New Techniques

Beading the Stem
Lacing

Three Cheery Spring Bulbs

Daffodil

6 petals
1 leaf
1 trumpet

What You Need for 1 Daffodil

2 hanks	11/0 transparent yellow beads for petals and trumpet
1 hank	11/0 transparent green beads for leaf and stem
1 spool	24-gauge gold wire for petals
1 spool	24-gauge green wire for leaf and for beading the stem
1 spool	30 to 34-gauge green lacing wire for leaves
1 spool	30 to 34-gauge gold assembly wire
2 pieces	18-gauge stem wire, wrapped in floral tape

Basic Flower-Making Kit

Making the Parts of the Daffodil

1 Make 6 petals. Pattern: 16-bead BF, 13 rows, PT, PB, reduce to 1 wire.

2 Make 1 trumpet. Pattern: 13 CL with 3½ inches of beads each. Leave 2 inches of bare wire on each side.

3 Make 1 leaf. Pattern: 3½-inch-bead BF, 9 rows, PT, PB, reduce to 3 wires. Use 6 inches of bare wire for bottom loop and leave 3 inches for top basic wire. Lace (see lacing instructions on page 54) in three places: 1½ inches from the top of the leaf, in the middle of the leaf, and 1½ inches from the bottom of the leaf.

PHOTO 1. WRAP ASSEMBLY WIRE
AROUND THE TOP ¼ INCH OF
EACH LOOP.

ASSEMBLING THE DAFFODIL

1 Straighten out the loops of the trumpet and make them as even as possible. Wrap assembly wire around the top ¼ inch of the first loop. Pull the wire tight to secure and wrap under and around the top ¼ inch of the next beaded loop. Again, gently pull the wire tight to bring the beaded loops together. Continue to the end. Wrap the wire around the last beaded loop twice to secure it. One side of the trumpet will have more wire showing than the other; this is the back side. Leave about 2 inches of wire and cut it. (See photo 1.)

2 Bring together the 2 wires at the beginning and end of the loops to form a circle. Keep the wire side of the trumpet facing in to the center of the circle. Weave 1 of the wires in and out of the loops halfway around the bottom of the structure. End with 1 wire opposite the other.

3 At the top of the trumpet, connect the beaded loops by weaving the assembly wire around from the last beaded loop to the first one. Continue wrapping around 2 or 3 loops or until the structure is secure.

4 To finish the trumpet, gently bend the top ¼ inch of each loop backward away from the center of the circle.

5 Add the petals.

6 Place the trumpet over the petals and insert 1 of its wires between 2 petals. Insert its opposite wire between the opposite petals. Gently pull the trumpet down so it is well seated in the center of the petals. Wrap with assembly wire to secure the trumpet to the stem wire.

7 With the tapestry needle threaded with assembly wire, weave the wire in between the petals and the trumpet to secure the structure. Make sure the wire is on the back side of the petals.

8 Bead the stem (see instructions on beading the stem on page 53) with green beaded wire. About 6 or 7 inches from the flower base, add the leaf and continue beading the stem.

Iris

3 petal units (1 upper petal +
   1 lower petal + 1 beard per unit)
1 leaf
1 stamen unit (3 stamens)

WHAT YOU NEED FOR 1 IRIS

2 hanks	11/0 purple or blue beads for petals
1 hank	11/0 green beads for leaf and stem
2 strands	11/0 yellow beads for beards and stamens
1 spool	24-gauge matching wire for petals
1 spool	24-gauge green wire for leaf and stem
1 spool	26-gauge gold wire for stamens and beards
1 spool	30 to 34-guage green lacing wire
2 pieces	18-gauge stem wire, wrapped in floral tape

Basic Flower-Making Kit

MAKING THE PARTS OF THE IRIS

1 Make 6 petals. Pattern: 16-bead BF, RT, PB, 15 rows, reduce to 1 wire.

2 The beards and the stamens are identical. Make 3 of each. Pattern: Make 1 loop with 1½ inches of beads. Leave 3 inches of bare wire on each side and twist together.

3 Make 1 leaf. Pattern: 2-½ inch-bead BF, RT, RB, 9 rows, reduce to 2 wires and twist. Lace in the middle. (See the lacing instructions on page 54.)

ASSEMBLING THE IRIS

1 Make the stamen unit by twisting together the 3 stamen wires under the beads.

2 Attach the stamen unit to the stem wires, so it extends about 2 inches above the stem.

3 Make 1 petal unit. Lay a beard on top of the front side (no wire showing) of a petal. Twist the wires together. Take the front side of another petal and lay it on top of the first petal and beard. (The wire side of both petals will be on the outside.) Twist together the wires of the 2 petals and the beard. (See photo 2.)

PHOTO 2. COMPLETE THE PETAL UNIT.

Take a 2-inch piece of the petal wire and loop it through both petals to secure the beard. Twist together the ends of this wire to secure the unit. With wire cutters, leave about ¼ inch of wire and turn it under. Make 2 more petal units.

4 Take 1 petal unit and hold the base of it (where the petals and the beard come together) to the top of the stem wires.

5 Secure the petal unit to the stem. Add the other 2 petal units evenly around the stem/stamen unit. (See photo 3.)

6 Bend the upper petals to the center over the stamens. Bend the tip of the lower petals down toward the stem. (See photo 4.)

7 Bead the stem with green beads (see the instructions below) and add the leaf.

PHOTO 3. HOLD THE BASE OF THE PETAL UNIT TO THE TOP OF THE STEM WIRES.

PHOTO 4. SHAPE THE PETALS WITH YOUR FINGERS.

Tulip

6 petals
1 leaf
5 stamens

WHAT YOU NEED FOR 1 TULIP

1 hank	11/0 red beads for petals
1 hank	11/0 transparent green beads for leaf and stem
2 strands	11/0 black beads for the stamen
1 spool	24-gauge red wire for petals
1 spool	24-gauge green wire for leaf and stem
1 spool	26-gauge black wire for stamens
2 pieces	18-gauge stem wires, wrapped in floral tape
1 spool	30 to 34-gauge red lacing wire for petals

Basic Flower-Making Kit

MAKING THE PARTS OF THE TULIP

1 See the reverse basic instructions in the Floating Gardenia project on page 47. Make 2 reverse basic petals. Pattern: 16-bead BF, 13 rows, reverse basic, reduce to 1 wire.

2 Make 4 basic frame petals. Pattern: 16-bead BF, 13 rows, reduce to 1 wire.

3 Make 1 leaf. Pattern: 3 ½-inch-bead BF, 9 rows, PT, PB, reduce to 3 wires. Lace (see instructions on page 54) in three places: 1½ inches from the top of the leaf, in the middle of the leaf, and 1½ inches from the bottom of the leaf.

4 Make 5 stamens. Pattern: Place 2 inches of black beads on 5 inches of wire. Clip from the spool and knot both ends. Push the

beads up to about ¾ inch of the end of the wire and make a small loop with 7 beads. Wrap the bare wire directly underneath the loop. Clip any excess wire close to the base of the loop, taking care not to allow any beads to slip off. Leave the rest of the beads on the wire.

ASSEMBLING THE TULIP

1 Take the 5 stamens and push their beads up toward the loops. Twist together the 5 stamens at the opposite end—this will keep any beads from slipping off. Cut the knots from the ends of the wires.

2 Attach the stamens (at the bottom of the beads) to the top of the stem wires.

3 Attach the 2 reverse basic petals so that the wire sides of the bottoms are facing in toward the stamens.

4 Attach the remaining 4 petals with the wire side facing in to the stamens.

5 Slightly bend the tips of the 2 reverse basic petals to the outside of the blossom. The slight bend will cover the top outside wire. The placement of the petals will give the tulip the appearance of opening up.

6 Using the lacing technique (see below), weave the petals together. Make sure the wire is on the inside of the blossom so it doesn't show. (If you wish, you can do this before you assemble on the stem. Lace together the 6 petals and then put the blossom on the stem.)

7 Wrap the stem with green beaded wire (see beading the stem instructions below.) About 6 or 7 inches from the flower base, add the leaf and continue beading the stem.

DESIGN TIP

Although the spring bulbs are gorgeous in a single shade, you may want to try a multicolored flower. You can make the trumpet of the daffodil a different color, or you can shade it (see the tipping on the loops technique in the Fancy Japanese Iris project on page 67). You can also shade the iris with some yellow beads in the center of the petals, making it look like the beards are actually growing out of the flower.

NEW TECHNIQUE

BEADING THE STEM

Beading the stem means that you wrap beaded wire around the stem of a flower to give it a finished look. It's particularly striking for flowers with thick stems.

1 From the spool of green beaded wire, take 1 inch of bare wire and press it lengthwise on the stem with the bottom of the wire pointed to the bottom of the stem, and the top of the wire as close to the flower base as possible. Then wrap the bare wire around the stem as close to the flower base as you can. Wrap the wire around again to secure it.

2 Push beads down to the base and begin to wrap the beaded

BEADING THE STEM MAKES THE ENTIRE FLOWER A LONG-STEMMED BEAUTY.

PHOTO 5. WRAP BEADED WIRE AROUND THE STEM.

wire around the stem. (See photo 5.) Continue about 8 inches down the stem. When you're finished, wrap the bare wire into the beaded stem 3 times and clip.

LACING

Lacing is a technique that you can use in many beaded flower projects to strengthen and add support to your petals and leaves. It's particularly helpful when you have a petal with lots of rows or a leaf with a long basic row. The technique uses a thin wire (30 to 34-gauge) threaded on a tapestry needle to hold the rows together, minimizing the amount of wire that shows. The lacing wire should match the color of the petal or leaf that you're lacing. Here's how to lace the leaves in this project.

1 Thread the tapestry needle with a 36-inch piece of 30 or 34-gauge green wire. Bend 1 inch of the wire down from the eye of the needle and twist it. This will keep the wire from coming out of the needle.

2 Hold the completed petal or leaf with the front facing you. Loop the wire twice around its right edge to lock it in place. You may find it easier to work from left to right, which is fine. (See photo 6.)

PHOTO 6. HERE'S HOW TO "SEW" A PETAL.

FIGURE 1. THE LACING TECHNIQUE HOLDS THE ROWS TOGETHER AND RESULTS IN WIRE SHOWING ON ONLY ONE SIDE OF THE LEAF. HERE'S LACING ON THE FRONT OF THE LEAF.

3 Bring the needle around to the back side of the petal or leaf and bring it up between the 2nd and 3rd rows. The laced element has a front (no wire showing) and a back side (wire showing). (See figures 1 and 2.)

4 Bring the needle over the 2nd row and down through the 1st and 2nd row.

5 Bring the needle up between the 3rd and 4th rows and then down between the 3rd and 2nd. Pull tightly, but not so tightly that you break the wire.

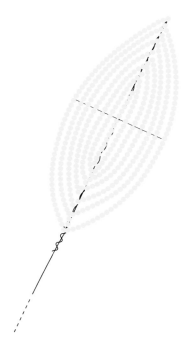

FIGURE 2. HERE'S LACING ON THE BACK OF THE LEAF.

6 As you sew across the petal or leaf, lock the wire in between the beads and try to keep your weaving in a straight line. Continue to the last row.

7 Loop around twice to lock the wire in place.

8 Clip the wire as close as you can.

Draping Wisteria

The wisteria vine makes any sturdy surface luxurious. Its raceme (or blossom) is made of 25 florets, each of which you'll make with two petals using the CWL technique. With florets in three sizes and two colors, the raceme turns slightly darker at its bottom. Each leaf is made of smaller leaflets. Amazing how many details of a flower you learn when you make a version of it in beads!

Basic Techniques

Basic Frame (BF)
Continuous Wraparound Loops (CWL)

1 Wisteria Raceme

(Note: There are 5 racemes in the 2-foot long vine in the project photograph. If you want to make all 5 racemes, be sure to multiply x 5 for the total number of parts.)

25 florets each

13 large florets (1 large + 1 medium petal for each floret = 26 petals)

10 medium florets (1 medium + 1 small petal for each floret = 20 petals)

2 small florets (2 small petals for each floret = 4 petals)

25 stamens

2 leaves with 7 to 9 leaflets

ANALYZING THE DETAILS OF A LIVE FLOWER IS THE SECRET TO
UNDERSTANDING HOW TO MAKE ITS BEADED VERSION.

WHAT YOU NEED
FOR 1 RACEME

(Note: To make 5 racemes, multiply x 5 for the
total amount of material needed.)

3 hanks	12/0 purple beads (color A) for large and medium petals
2 hanks	12/0 darker purple (color B) for small petals
3 hanks	11/0 green beads for leaves
3 strands	12/0 yellow beads for stamens
1 spool	26-gauge purple wire for florets
1 spool	24-gauge green wire for leaves
1 spool	28-gauge gold wire for stamens
1 spool	22-gauge green wire or other pliable stiff wire for vine

Thumbtacks or nails, as needed,
  to hold or hang the
  completed branch
Basic Flower-Making Kit

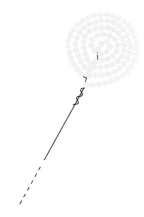

FIGURE 1. THE WISTERIA PETAL HAS 3
WRAPAROUND LOOPS.

MAKING THE PARTS OF
1 RACEME

1 With color A, make 13 large
petals for large florets. Pattern:
Make 1 wraparound loop, with a
total of 5 loops, beginning with 6
beads. Leave 1½ inches of bare
wire on 1 side. Clip the spool wire
close to the twist, leaving a single
wire stem. (See figure 1.)

2 With color A, make 23 medium
petals for large and medium
florets. Pattern: Make 1 wraparound loop, with a total of 4
loops, beginning with 6 beads.
Leave 1½ inches of bare wire on
one side. Clip the wire close to the
twist, leaving a single wire stem

3 With color B, make 14 small
petals for small florets.
Pattern: Make 1 wraparound loop,
with a total of 3 loops, beginning
with 6 beads. Leave 1½ inches of
bare wire on one side. Clip the
wire close to the twist, leaving a
single wire stem

4 Make 25 stamens, 1 for each floret. Pattern: On 28-or higher gauge wire, make a simple loop with 5 to 7 beads. Leave 2 inches of bare wire on each side and twist the wires tightly for 1 inch.

5 Make 16 leaflets for 2 leaves (7 leaflets for 1 leaf, 9 for the other). Pattern: ¾-inch-bead BF, PT, RB, 7 rows, reduce to 1 wire. Vary the leaflets in size by making the center or basic row a little longer or shorter to make the leaf look more natural. Use flat-nose pliers to tighten the wires at the base of each leaflet, and cover the leaflet stem with floral tape.

6 Repeat all the above steps to complete the remaining 4 racemes that will make up the 5 racemes for the vine branch.

ASSEMBLING THE WISTERIA VINE BRANCH

1 Make 13 large florets. For each floret, place the stamen on the wire side of the large petal. Take a medium petal and place the wire side over the stamen. Tightly twist together the 3 wires of the two petals and the stamen. The floret will look like a clam. After the wires are twisted, open up the floret.

2 Make 10 medium florets. For each one, take 1 medium petal (color A), 1 small petal (color B), and 1 stamen and twist together the wires as in step 1.

3 Make 2 small florets. For each one, take 2 small petals (color B) and 1 stamen and twist together the wires as in step 1.

4 Cut an 8-inch length of floral tape in half lengthwise. Cover the stem of each floret with a half-width of floral tape. Cut more floral tape as you need it.

5 Form the cone shape of the raceme by adding and building on the florets. (See figure 1.) Twist together the wires of the 2 smallest florets. These will form the tip of the raceme and also the stem for the raceme. Add the medium, then the larger florets by twisting together the wires of all the florets. Use jaw-nose or flat-nose pliers to twist the wire. Make the raceme wider at the top than at the bottom. The pattern calls for 25 florets for each raceme. Add a few more or less florets to vary the shape and size.

6 The leaves are clustered in odd numbers (7 to 9) of leaflets. There is a center leaflet at the top and an even number of leaflets on the side. For each raceme, add 2 or 3 pairs of leaflets. To make a leaf, attach the leaflets to each other by twisting together the wires. Use 1 leaflet as the center. Leave about ½ to 1 inch of stem showing and, with floral tape, attach 1 pair of leaflets ½ inch from the base of the center leaf. Continue wrapping with floral tape and add another pair ½ inch from the first pair. (See figure 2.) Make the second leaf with 1 center and 3 pairs of leaflets (7 leaflets).

7 Cut a piece of the 22-gauge wire the length of your vine and cover it with floral tape. Lay the leaf on top of the wire and attach it with the tape. Add the second leaf about 1 or 1½ inches from the first. Add the raceme. Continue adding leaves and racemes until you have the desired length.

PHOTO 1. FORM THE RACEME BY ADDING FLORETS.

FIGURE 2. THE WISTERIA LEAF IS COMPRISED OF A CENTER LEAFLET AND 2 PAIRS OF LEAFLETS.

USE THUMBTACKS OR NAILS TO CREATE THE DRAPE OF THE WISTERIA VINE ACROSS THE FRAME OF A MIRROR.

Anemone Accessory

Anemones, or windflowers, come in all sizes, shapes, and colors. This one is small and sweet, a perfect hair ornament if you're young or young at heart. It has five white petals, each one outlined with pink. Fashion your personal anemone with any colors you like by using the simple outlining technique.

Basic Techniques

Basic Frame (BF)
Continuous Loops (CL)

New Technique

Outlining

Anemone

5 petals
1 leaf
1 calyx
6 stamens

What You Need for 1 Anemone

1 hank	11/0 or 12/0 beads (color A) for petals (any color you wish, I used white)
1 hank	11/0 or 12/0 beads (contrasting color B) to outline petals (any color you wish, I used pink)
1 hank	11/0 green beads for leaf and calyx
1 strand	11/0 gold beads for stamens
1 spool	26-gauge colored wire for petals
1 spool	24-gauge green wire for leaf and calyx
1 spool	26-gauge gold wire for stamens
1 barrette or hair comb	
Basic Flower-Making Kit	

Making the Parts of the Anemone

1. Make 5 petals with color A. Pattern: 5-bead BF, RT, PB, 11 rows, reduce to 1 wire. See outlining instructions on page 60 and outline the last 2 rows with contrasting color B.

2. Make the leaf. Pattern: 4-bead BF, PT, RB, 11 rows, reduce to 1 wire.

3. Make the calyx. Pattern: Make 7 CL with 1 inch of beads each. Leave 2 inches of bare wire on each side.

4. Make 6 stamens. Push 3 gold beads up to within 3 inches of the end of the wire. Begin twisting the wire right below the beads for about 2 inches.

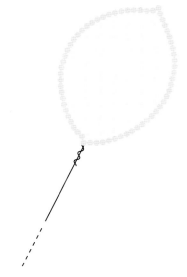

Figure 1. Outlining the last 2 rows of the petal in a contrasting color makes both colors pop.

USE THE OUTLINING TECHNIQUE TO ADD
VISUAL INTEREST TO THE PETALS OR
LEAVES OF ANY FLOWER.

ASSEMBLING THE ANEMONE

1 Two inches below the beads, twist together the 6 stamens to form a stem.

2 With assembly wire, add each of the petals at the point where the stamens are twisted together. With nylon jaw-nose or flat-nose pliers, carefully twist together the wires of the stem.

3 Add the calyx.

4 Add the leaf under the calyx.

5 With assembly wire, attach the completed flower to the barrette or comb. Or place the flower in your hair and hold it with sturdy bobby pins.

DESIGN TIP

Take any flower and modify it for a hat or handbag. Instead of assembling the flower on a long stem wire, use the wires of the stamen or center as a short stem.

NEW TECHNIQUE

OUTLINING

Outlining a petal or a leaf in a different color adds interest to the flower. Look at the petals in the Striped Tiger Lily project on page 100 and the Loving Roses on page 89, which were outlined with a color similar to the petal color. In the anemone, you'll use a contrasting color to highlight the color of the petal. The techniques are the same.

1 Estimate the amount of wire you'll need for the last 2 rows of the petal or leaf you want to shade. (In the case of the anemone, this would be after you've beaded 9 rows of the petal.) Add 6 inches and clip this amount of bare wire from the spool.

2 Place enough color B beads on the wire to complete 2 rows. Finish the petals and clip the extra wire from the frame. (See figure 1 on page 59.)

Butterfly-Kissed Geranium

One sure way to make a house a home is with a pot of bright red geraniums. Its blossoms are composed of dozens of florets made easily with continuous wraparound loops. A new technique—split loop—results in leaves with notched ends where they're attached to the stem. Perch a charming butterfly where everyone can see it.

Basic Techniques

Basic Frame (BF)
Continuous Wraparound Loops (CWL)

New Technique

Split Loop

Geranium

4 blossoms (2 small with
   16 florets each and 2 large
   with 24 florets each)
48 leaves (small, medium, large,
   and extra-large)

WHAT YOU NEED FOR 1 GERANIUM

3 hanks	11/0 or 12/0 red beads for blossoms
5 hanks	11/0 green beads for leaves
1 spool	26-gauge red wire for blossoms
3 spools	24-gauge green wire for leaves
1 spool	30-gauge green lacing wire for leaves
1 piece	wire coat hanger or similar wire for main stem, cut to 12 inches and wrapped with floral tape
3 pieces	18-gauge stem wire for secondary stems, cut to 5 to 7-inch lengths and wrapped with floral tape

Terra-cotta planter or other pot at least 4 inches deep

Floral clay

Dried moss

Basic Flower-Making Kit

MAKING THE PARTS OF THE GERANIUM

1 Make 80 florets, 32 for 2 small blossoms (16 for each) and 48 for 2 large blossoms (24 for each). Pattern for each floret: Make 4 CWL, 2 loops each, beginning with an 8-bead loop. Leave 4 inches of bare wire on each side. Tightly twist together the ends, leaving a 3½-inch stem. It's not necessary to cover the stem. (Refer to photo 1 and figure 1.)

PHOTO 1. WRAP ASSEMBLY WIRE AROUND FLORETS TO FORM A CLUSTER.

2 See the split loop instructions on page 65. You'll use this technique for all 4 sizes of leaves. Make 8 small leaves. Pattern: 6-bead BF, RT, RB, 4 rows, split the loop and add 3 double rows on each side, finish on the right bottom loop for a total of 17 rows.

3 Make 10 medium leaves. Pattern: 8-bead BF, RT, RB, 8 rows, split the loop and add 3 double rows on each side, finish on the right bottom loop for a total of 21 rows. Every time you finish a leaf, including in the following steps, use your fingers to mold the edges to create a slight ruffled effect.

4 Make 10 large leaves. Pattern: 8-bead BF, RT, RB, 6 rows, split the loop and add 4 double rows on each side, finish on the right bottom loop for 25 rows.

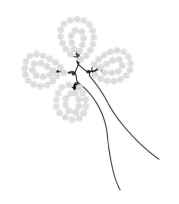

FIGURE 1. THE GERANIUM FLORET HAS 4 CWLS.

5 Make 20 extra-large leaves. Pattern: 8-bead BF, RT, RB, 6 rows, split the loop and add 5 double rows on each side, finish on the right bottom loop for 27 rows.

ASSEMBLING THE GERANIUM

1 Make 2 large blossoms with 24 florets each. Place 1 floret about ½ inch above the tip of the main stem and wrap it 2 or 3 times with assembly wire. Add around it the 23 remaining florets to create a ball shape. Keep the petals of each floret facing out to give the blossom a full look and also hide the wires. (See photo 1 on page 62.)

2 Assemble the second large blossom on a secondary stem.

3 Make 2 small blossoms with 16 florets each. Use a secondary stem for each and assemble the florets in the same manner as the large blossom.

4 With floral tape, attach 7 or 8 leaves of different sizes under the blossoms on each of the 3 secondary stems. Place the smaller leaves close to the base of the blossom and the larger leaves at the bottom of the stem. Leave

at least 3 inches of taped wire at the bottom.

5 With floral tape, attach the secondary stems with their blossoms and leaves to the main stem. Leave 5 inches of taped wire at the bottom in order to have a substantial "stem" to plant. Add the remainder of the leaves to fill in any bare spots.

6 Fill a planter with floral clay and plant your geranium. Bend the leaves and branches to make them look real. Cover the floral clay with a little dried moss.

DESIGN TIP

By changing the number of florets, you can also make your blossoms bigger or smaller and more or less round. Make several plants, of different colors, and put them in a window box.

Butterfly

2 large wings
2 small wings
2 antennae
1 body

WHAT YOU NEED FOR 1 BUTTERFLY

I used gold beads and wire for the butterfly on the homey geranium to give it a surprising dash of glitter. If you wish to make brightly colored butterfly wings, use black beads for the body and the antennae to accentuate the colors.

1 hank	11/0 colored beads for wings
1 hank	11/0 colored beads for body and antennae
1 spool	24-gauge wire for wings
1 spool	26-gauge wire for body and antennae
1 spool	30 to 34-gauge assembly wire

Basic Flower-Making Kit

FIGURE 2. WRAP A STRING OF BEADED WIRE AROUND THE ANTENNAE TO FORM THE BODY.

MAKING THE PARTS OF THE BUTTERFLY

1 Make 2 large wings. Pattern: Push 12 beads to within 1½ inches of the end of the wire and make a loop. Make 2 wraparound loops. Begin the 4th loop and, halfway around, take 10 beads and twist into a loop. This will form a point on the wing. Continue to wrap the beads around in the normal way to finish the loop. Twist around the base wire. For the 5th wraparound loop, wrap the beads around the 4th loop, including around the point. Bend the beaded wire to shape the wing. Twist the spool wire with the end wire and clip. You should have about 1½ inches of twisted and bare wire.

2 Make 2 small wings. Pattern: Push 12 beads to within 1½ inches of the end of the wire and make a loop. Make 1 wrap-around loop. Twist to secure the wires.
Begin the 3rd loop and wrap the beads halfway around. Take 10 beads and twist into a loop. This makes the fancy tip on the small wing. Finish wrapping the loop to complete the wing. Twist the spool wire with the end wire and clip. You should have about 1½ inches of twisted and bare wire.

3 Make 2 antennae with eyes. String 3 beads onto 3½ inches of bare wire. Push the beads to the middle of the wire. Hold the 2 wires under the beads and twist them tightly together for about 1½ inches.

4 Hold the 2 antennae together. About ½ inch from the eyes, begin to twist together the two antennae. Twist for 1½ inches. The twisted wire will provide the core of the body.

5 Make the body. String 5 inches of gold beads on wire. Beginning at the point where the antennae are joined, wrap the beaded wire around the antennae, just as you would bead the stem of the Daffodil (page 53). When you get to the end, wrap the bare wire around itself and clip. (See figure 2.)

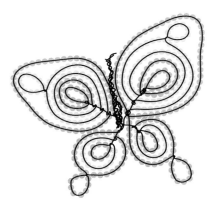

FIGURE 3. TWIST THE LARGE AND SMALL WINGS TOGETHER.

ASSEMBLING THE BUTTERFLY

1 Twist together the end wires of the 2 large wings.

2 Twist together the end wires of the 2 small wings.

3 Bend the wires of both sets of wings perpendicular to the right side (no wire showing) of the wings. With jaw-nose or flat-nose pliers, twist the wires together. Carefully bend the twisted wires to the center of the wings on the right side. Flatten the wire and press as close as you can to the wings. Leave about ½ inch of twisted wire and clip. Be careful not to clip too much! (See figure 3.)

4 Place the body over the twisted wires in the center of the wings. Use assembly wire to attach the body to the wings. Press the wire in between the rows on the body so the wire doesn't show.

5 Place the butterfly on the flower, using assembly wire to secure it, if needed.

DESIGN TIP

Using the shading technique (see the Flowering Dogwood project, page 80), color butterflies with reds, yellows, blues, and oranges. Add a pin or barrette to the butterfly to make a charming accessory.

NEW TECHNIQUE

SPLIT LOOP

The split loop technique gives the geranium leaf the notched end at its base. Other flowers such as the dogwood also use this technique.

1 Start a 6-bead BF, RT and RB as you normally would. Complete 4 rows (basic row plus 3). The spool wire will be at the top of the frame. (See figure 4.)

2 With the wire cutters, split the bottom loop in the center and straighten out the wires. You now have 3 wires on the basic frame, 1 at the top (basic wire) and 2 at the bottom.

3 With the front side facing you, take the beaded spool wire down the right side, wrap around the right split loop, and come back up the right side. Loop completely around the basic wire and, with the front facing you, go down the left side of the leaf. Loop the beaded wire completely around the left split loop. Go back up to the basic wire and wrap completely around. You have now completed 1 double row on the right and the left side of the leaf. (See figure 5.)

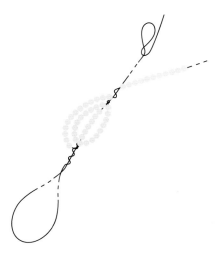

FIGURE 4. YOU'VE COMPLETED THE FIRST 4 ROWS AND ARE READY TO SPLIT THE BOTTOM LOOP.

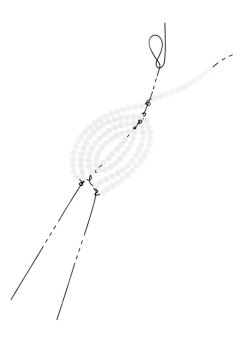

FIGURE 5. YOU'VE NOW COMPLETED 1 DOUBLE ROW ON EACH SIDE OF THE BASIC ROW AND ARE READY TO START ROWS 9 AND 10 ON THE RIGHT SIDE OF THE LEAF.

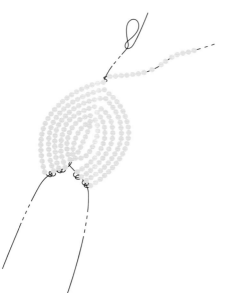

FIGURE 6. YOU'VE NOW COMPLETED 2 DOUBLE ROWS ON EACH SIDE OF THE BASIC ROW AND ARE READY TO START ROWS 13 AND 14 ON THE RIGHT SIDE OF THE LEAF.

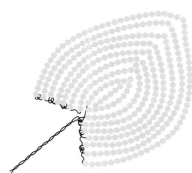

FIGURE 7. THE SPLIT LOOP TECHNIQUE RESULTS IN A COMPLETED LEAF WITH 17 ROWS AND A NOTCH AT ITS STEM.

4 Go down the right side of the frame and wrap around the right split loop and back to the top basic wire. Wrap around the top basic wire and go down to the left split loop. Wrap around the left split loop and return to the top basic. You have now completed 2 double rows. (See figure 6.)

5 Continue until you have completed 3 double loops on each side. You'll be at the top basic. Bring the beaded wire to the right split loop and loop it around the wire several times. You should have 17 rows. (See figure 7.)

6 Clip the wire from the spool. Bend each of the 2 loop wires onto the back of the leaf and weave the ends of the wire through the center of the bottom of the leaf. Twist the 2 wires together to make the stem of the leaf. Clip the top basic wire and bend to the back of the leaf.

Fancy Japanese Iris

The fancy Japanese iris—with its five petals, many leaves, and flamboyant center—craves the spotlight. You'll add dramatic flair by using two new techniques: ruffling the edges of the petals and tipping their loops.

Basic Techniques

Basic Frame (BF)
Continuous Loops (CL)

Special Techniques

Lacing

New Techniques

Ruffling
Tipping the Loops

Fancy Japanese Iris

5 petals
1 bud
14 leaves of varied sizes
1 inner center
1 outer center
10 sepals

What You Need for 1 Fancy Japanese Iris

1 hank	11/0 or 12/0 (color A) beads for petals, inner center and bud (any color, I used light blue)
1 hank	11/0 or 12/0 (color B) beads for petals, inner center and bud (any color, I used dark blue)
4 hanks	11/0 green beads for leaves and sepals
1 strand	11/0 or 12/0 yellow beads for outer center
1 spool	26-gauge colored wire for petals, inner center and bud
1 spool	24-gauge green wire for leaves and sepals
1 spool	26-gauge gold wire for outer center
1 spool	30 to 34-gauge green wire to lace leaves
1 piece	wire coat hanger or similar size wire for the blossom stem, cut to 14 inches and wrapped with floral tape
14 pieces	18-gauge stem wires for leaf stems, cut to 4 inch-lengths
1 piece	18-gauge stem wire for the bud stem, cut to 6 inches and wrapped with floral tape

Floral clay
Shallow round bowl
Dried moss
Floral marbles
Basic Flower-Making Kit

UP CLOSE YOU CAN CLEARLY SEE THE EXCITING EFFECTS CREATED BY THE TECHNIQUES OF RUFFLING AND TIPPING ON THE LOOPS

Making the Parts of the Fancy Japanese Iris

1 See the instructions on pages 69-70 for the two new techniques of ruffling and tipping on the loops. You'll use these techniques for the petals and inner center. Make 5 petals beginning with color A. Pattern: 10-bead BF, PT, PB, 7 rows. At the beginning of row 6, make a ruffle (see instructions on page 69) with random-sized loops ranging in size from 1 to 4 inches of beaded wire. Shade the tips of the ruffle loops (see instructions) with Color B according to the pattern in figure 1 on page 70.

2 Make the inner center with Color A. Make 16 CL with 5 to 7 inches of beads each. Leave 2 inches of bare wire on either side. Tip the edges of each loop with color B.

3 Press the sides of each loop together so the loop is straight. You'll have a strip of loops from 2½ to 3 inches each. About 2 inches from the bottom of the loops, use assembly wire and lace the first loop to the second, the second to the third and so on. (See the lacing instructions in the Three Cheery Spring Bulbs project on page 54—this is similar to making the daffodil trumpet. You'll also lace in step

8 below.) Pull the wire tight after connecting each loop. After you connect the 15th to the 16th loop, with the wire side facing out, connect the 16th loop to the 1st loop. You now have a circle of uneven loops.

4 Gently bend the top of each loop away from the center of the circle. Twist the loops as you did with the petals in step 1 to create a natural look.

5 Make the outer center. Pattern: Make 20 CL, beginning with 1 to 1½ inches each. Leave 2 inches of bare wire on each side.

6 Make 10 sepals, 5 for the blossom and 5 for the bud. Pattern: 15-bead BF, RT, RB, 7 rows, reduce to 1 wire.

7 Make the bud. Pattern: With colors A and B, make 12 CL with 3½ to 5 inches of beads each. Tip the edges of the loops as you did in step 1. Curl the loops together, as if you were rolling them like mini-rugs.

8 Make 14 leaves of different sizes by varying the length of the basic row and the number of rows. Pattern: 3 to 5-inch-bead BF, PT, PB, 9 to 13 rows, reduce to 3 wires and twist the wires together. Lace in the middle of the petal and at the top and bottom if necessary. With floral tape, attach a 4-inch piece of stem wire to each leaf. When making the BF for the larger leaves, particularly those with a 4 or 5-inch-bead basic, leave about 4 inches of bare wire at the top. Make the bottom loop with about 8 inches of wire. Because these are big leaves, and both ends are pointed, you'll need extra wire

on the basic frames on which to wrap the beads.

ASSEMBLING THE FANCY JAPANESE IRIS

1 Attach the inner center at the top of the coat hanger stem.

2 Add the outer center around the base of the inner center.

3 Add the petals at right angles to the center and keep the wire side of the petals facing down.

4 Add 5 sepals under the petals.

5 Bead the stem with green beads. (See the beading the stem instructions in the Three Cheery Spring Bulbs project on page 53. You'll also bead the stem in Step 9.)

6 Attach the bud to the top of the 6-inch bud stem.

7 Attach 5 sepals on the stem around the bud, covering about two-thirds of the loops of the bud.

8 Bead the bud stem just as you did the main stem.

9 Soften the floral clay with your hands and push it into the bowl, spreading it to the edges. Plant the Japanese iris by pushing the main stem about 2 inches into the clay or until it feels secure. Insert the smaller bud stem. Surround these two stems with leaf stems, trimming the leaves as necessary before inserting them into the clay. Cover the clay with moss to hide all the wires, and then add a few floral marbles.

DESIGN TIP

You can make this flower in any combination of colors. Blue with orange edges would be spectacular, as would fiery red with yellow edges.

NEW TECHNIQUE

RUFFLING

Adding a ruffle to a petal gives it extra excitement—and don't worry, it's not as hard as it looks. On the last two rows of the basic frame, you'll make a strip of continuous loops. These loops can all be the same size—or they can have loops of varying sizes like the Fancy Japanese Iris. Here are instructions specific to that flower.

THIS CATTLEYA ORCHID BY ROSEMARY TOPOL SHOWS OFF THE RUFFLING TECHNIQUE.

1 You'll start and end the CL strip with a 1-inch loop. The center loop is the longest loop (about 2 inches or 4 inches of beads), and when wrapped around the petal, it will be at the top point. You'll make 22 to 28 loops, depending on the size of your beads.

2 Twist the tip of each loop in a slightly different direction. After you've made all the loops, finish the BF by wrapping the CL strip around the top basic wire (completing row 6) and around the bottom twist (completing row 7).

3 Wrap bare wire around the bottom and twist 3 times to secure the petal. Reduce to 3 wires and twist them together. Wasn't that easy?

New Technique

TIPPING ON THE LOOPS

This technique is based on the same principle as tipping the edges on a basic frame in the Glass House Dahlia project on page 41. In this case, you tip, or shade with a different color, on the edges of loops of a ruffle.

1 Cut about 3 yards of bare wire from the spool and bead the wire as you make your loops. For example, in the Fancy Japanese Iris, for the first 4 loops, use all one color. For the 5th loop, bead about ½ inch of Color A, then ½ inch of Color B, and then another ½ inch of Color A. This will create a 1½-inch loop. The top ¼ inch will be tipped with Color B.

2 For the next loop, add ¾ inch of Color A, ½ to ¾ inch of Color B, and then another ¾ inch of Color A. This will create a slightly larger loop. You don't have to be exact—the randomness of your color variation adds vibrancy. (See figure 1.)

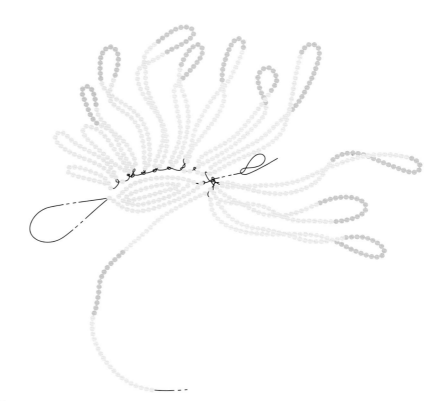

FIGURE 1. ROW 6 OF THE PETAL SHOWS A SERIES OF CONTINUOUS LOOPS WITH SHADED TIPS.

Party Perfect Peony

Worn on a simple hat, handbag, or wide belt, this sparkly amethyst peony is a perfect fashion accent. The leaf pattern is similar to one I saw in Godey's Ladies Magazine from the 1850s. It uses bugle beads instead of seed beads, with the same continuous wraparound loops technique as the petals. Making two colors of petals adds to their appeal.

Basic Technique

Continuous Wraparound Loops
   (CWL)

Peony

5 petal units (2 with Color A,
   3 with Color B)
1 small leaf with 7 leaflets
1 larger leaf with 7 leaflets
1 calyx

What You Need for 1 Peony

1 hank	11/0 beads (Color A) for petal units 1 and 2 (any color, I used light amethyst)
2 hanks	11/0 beads (Color B) for petal units 3, 4, and 5 (any color, I used dark amethyst)
1 hank	11/0 short bugle beads for leaves
1 hank	11/0 green beads for calyx
1 spool	24-gauge wire for petals
1 spool	24-gauge green wire for leaves and calyx
1 pin back	or needle and thread to attach flower to hat
Basic Flower-Making Kit	

Making the Parts of the Peony

1 Make 5 petal units, each as a strip of 3 CWL, with 3 inches of bare wire on each side.

- **Petal Unit 1**
  With color A beads, make 3 CWL, 4 loops each, beginning with a 16-bead loop. Leave ¼ inch of bare wire between the loops

- **Petal Unit 2**
  With color A beads, make 3 CWL, 5 loops each, beginning with a 17-bead loop. Leave ¼ inch of bare wire between the loops.

- **Petal Unit 3**
  With color B beads, make 3 CWL, 6 loops each, beginning with an 18-bead loop. Leave ½ inch of bare wire between the loops. (See figure 1.)

- **Petal Unit 4**
  With color B beads, make 3 CWL, 7 loops each, beginning with a 20-bead loop. Leave ½ inch of bare wire between the loops.

- **Petal Unit 5**
  With color B beads, make 3 CWL, 8 loops each, beginning with a 23-bead loop. Leave ½ inch of bare wire between the loops.

2 Make the calyx with seed beads (or bugle beads, if you wish.) Pattern: Make 5 CWL, 3 loops each, beginning with a 1½-inch loop. Before adding the 2nd and 3rd loops, squeeze together the 1st loop to form a point. As you wrap the 2nd and 3rd loops, create a point at the top. Leave 3 inches of bare wire on each side.

3 Make 1 small leaf with 7 leaflets. Pattern: Make a 1-inch loop with seed or bugle beads. Squeeze the sides of the loop together to lengthen it. Wrap the end wire around it again to secure it and clip. Add a pair of 1-inch loops under the 1st loop. These are the first 3 leaflets. Push ½ inch of beads up to the bottom of the 3 leaflets to create the stem. Add another pair of leaflets, adding 1 wraparound loop to each. Push ½ inch of beads to the base of the leaflets to make the stem. Make 1 more pair of leaflets in the same manner. Push 1½ inches of beads to the base of the leaflets to make a stem. Leave about 2 inches of bare wire. Clip from the spool and make a knot at the end of the bare wire to keep the beads from falling off. (See figure 2.)

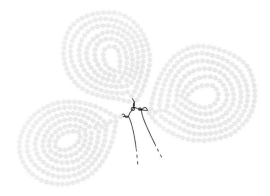

Figure 1. A petal unit for the peony is comprised of 3 sets of CWL. Each set has a simple loop and 5 wraparound loops.

Figure 2. Simple loops form the top of the peony leaf; pairs of leaflets made from wraparound loops are placed down the stem.

I USED THIS VINTAGE FLOWER THAT I FOUND IN AN ANTIQUE SHOP TO
MAKE THE PATTERN FOR THE PEONY IN THIS PROJECT. OVER HALF A
CENTURY OLD AND STILL GORGEOUS!

4 Make 1 large leaf with 7 leaflets.
This leaf is similar to the small
leaf, but the second and third pairs
of leaflets have 2 wraparound loops
each. You'll also start each leaflet
with a slightly larger loop: 1½ inches of seed beads or bugle beads.

ASSEMBLING THE PEONY

1 Take petal unit 1 and bring
together the ends to form a
circle. Twist the ends to form a stem.

2 Wrap petal unit 2 around petal
unit 1. Twist the wires together
2 or 3 times to hold them in place.

3 Repeat step 2 with petal
units 3 through 5 to complete
the blossom.

4 With nylon jaw-nose pliers
(or your fingers), tightly twist
together all of the wires to form
the stem.

5 Add the calyx.

6 Bead the stem (see the Three
Cheery Spring Bulbs project on
page 53) and add the leaves.

7 Attach the flower to a hat with a
pin back (see the Classic Poppy
Pin project on page 33), or sew it
on with a needle and sturdy thread.

DESIGN TIP

Experiment with a variety of colors
to produce multicolored peonies.
Use 3 or even 4 shades of a color,
making each unit a different shade.
You can use this technique to give
exciting dimension to any flower
with multiple big petals, such as
roses, poinsettias, and gardenias.

Summer Perennials

Shout out the joys of summer with a display of pointy-petaled perennials. A quartet of continuous loops gives the echinacea its riotous center; the dome technique rounds the black-eyed Susan's center like a licorice gumdrop. Fancy up the flowers with ferns and a bejeweled bumblebee.

ECHINACEA DESIGN BY MELISSA ELLIS

Basic Techniques

Basic Frame (BF)
Continuous Crossover Loops (CCL)
Continuous Loops (CL)

Special Techniques

Beading the Stem
Lacing

New Techniques

Dome

Black-Eyed Susan

11 petals
3 leaves
1 center
1 calyx

WHAT YOU NEED FOR 1 BLACK-EYED SUSAN

2 hanks	11/0 yellow beads for petals
1 hank	11/0 green beads for leaves and calyx
2 strands	11/0 black beads for center
1 spool	24-gauge gold wire for petals
1 spool	24-gauge green wire for leaves and calyx
1 spool	24-gauge black wire for center
2 pieces	18-gauge stem wire, wrapped with floral tape

Basic Flower-Making Kit

MAKING THE PARTS OF THE BLACK-EYED SUSAN

1 Make 11 petals. Pattern: 20-bead BF, PT, PB, reduce to 1 wire.

2 Make 1 center. Pattern: 6-bead BF, RT, RB, 11 rows. Create a dome shape beginning at row 4 (see dome instructions on page 79.) Twist the bottom 2 inches of the wires together. Push the upper wires inside the dome. This will leave a twisted wire protruding from the dome that will be attached to the stem wire.

3 Make 1 calyx. Pattern: 5 CCL beginning with a 3-inch loop of beads. Leave 2 inches of bare wire on each side.

4 Make 3 leaves. Pattern: 4-bead BF, PT, RB, 13 rows, reduce to 2 wires and twist together.

ASSEMBLING THE BLACK-EYED SUSAN

1 Attach the dome to the top of the stem.

2 Add the petals.

3 Add the calyx.

4 Begin beading the stem (see instructions in the Three Cheery Spring Bulbs project on page 53) and add the leaves about 2, 3, and 4 inches below the blossom.

Echinacea

15 petals
5 leaves (2 small, 2 medium, 1 large)
4 centers (1 very small, 1 small, 1 medium, 1 large)

WHAT YOU NEED FOR 1 ECHINACEA

2 hanks	11/0 pink beads for petals and centers.
2 hanks	11/0 green beads for leaves and stem
1 tube	6/0 green beads for the center row of the leaf
1 hank	11/0 yellow beads for very small center (stamens)
1 spool	26-gauge colored wire for petals and medium and large centers
1 spool	24-gauge green wire for leaves
1 spool	28-gauge gold wire for very small center (stamens)
2 pieces	18-gauge stem wire, wrapped in floral wire
1 spool	30 to 34-gauge green lacing wire for the large leaf

Basic Flower-Making Kit

MAKING THE PARTS OF THE ECHINACEA

1 Make 15 petals. Pattern: 1½-inch-bead BF, PT, PB, 5 rows, reduce to 1 wire. Before you begin row 4, clip off the knot on the top basic wire and add 2 pink beads. Wrap rows 4 and 5 around these 2 beads. This will create a very pointy end. (See figure 1.)

2 Make 1 very small center (the stamen) with yellow beads and 28-gauge wire. Pattern: 12 CL with 5 beads each. Leave 2 inches of bare wire on each side in this step and for the following steps 3 through 5.

3 Make 1 small center with pink beads and 26-gauge wire. Pattern: 20 CL with 1 inch of beads each.

4 Make 1 medium center with pink beads and 26-gauge wire. Pattern: 20 CL with 1½ inches of beads each.

5 Make 1 large center with pink beads and 26-gauge wire. Pattern: 25 CL with 2 inches of beads each.

6 Make 2 small leaves. Pattern: 2-inch-bead BF, PT, PB, 9 rows, reduce to 1 wire. Use size 6/0 beads for the basic row and size 11/0 beads for all the remaining rows. This will provide extra support for the long leaf. (See figure 2.)

7 Make 2 medium leaves. Pattern: 2½ inch-bead BF, PT, PB, 9 rows, reduce to 1 wire. Use the size 6/0 beads for the basic row and the size 11/0 beads for all the remaining rows.

FIGURE 1. ADDING 2 BEADS ON THE BASIC WIRE MAKES THE PETAL VERY POINTED.

8 Make 1 large leaf. Pattern: 3-inch-bead BF, PT, PB, 9 rows, reduce to 1 wire. Use the size 6/0 beads for the basic row and the size 11/0 beads for all the remaining rows. Lace the leaf as needed (see lacing instructions on page 54).

ASSEMBLING THE ECHINACEA

1 Curl or coil the loops of the very small center. Attach to the stem.

2 Attach 1 end wire of the small center directly underneath the stamens. Take the other end of wire and wrap it around the stem wires as tightly as you can and then secure the 2nd end wire with assembly wire. Wrapping the loops in this fashion will create a more organic and random effect than would using 3 layers of single wraps.

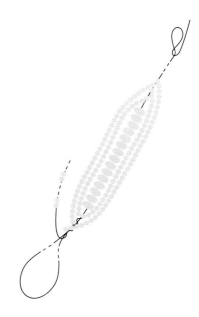

FIGURE 2. THE ECHINACEA LEAF HAS A BASIC ROW OF SIZE 6/0 BEADS.

3 Repeat step 2 with the medium and large centers.

4 Add the petals.

5 Bead the stem (see instructions in the Three Cheery Spring Bulbs project on page 54) and add the leaves at various points along the stem.

6 Shape the flower by "fluffing" the center petals with your fingers and curving the lower petals so that the top of each lower petal rests up against the bottom of the center petal.

Bumblebee

Body
2 wings

WHAT YOU NEED FOR 1 BUMBLEBEE

2 strands	11/0 black beads for body
1 strand	11/0 yellow beads for body
1 strand	11/0 crystal beads for wings
1 spool	28-gauge gold wire for body
1 spool	28-gauge white wire for wings

Basic Flower-Making Kit

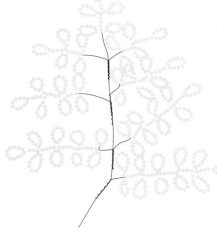

FIGURE 3. HERE'S ONE WAY TO MAKE FERNS.

MAKING THE FERNS AND FOLIAGE

In beaded flowers there aren't any rules about how to make ferns and other common foliage, so use your imagination. You can make a series of small continuous loops and then attach them to a stem, or you can use large loops. Usually ferns are placed around the outside of the arrangement or used as filler to round out a bouquet. The amount will vary depending on how many flowers you make. (See figure 3.)

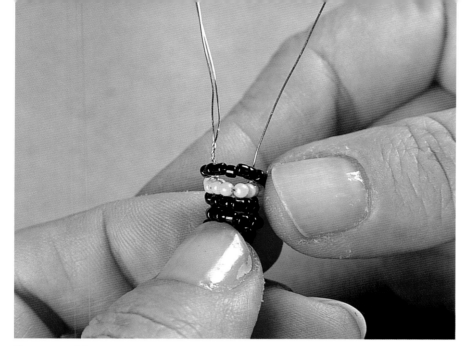

PHOTO 1. MAKE ALTERNATE ROWS OF YELLOW AND BLACK BEADS.

MAKING THE PARTS OF THE BEE

1 Make the body. Pattern: With black beads, make a 20-bead BF, and complete 3 black rows. Measure about 20 inches of bare wire and clip it from the spool. Bend the top basic wire and bottom loop 90(. Using the dome technique (below at right), add 2 more rows in black (rows 4 and 5). (See photo 1.) Add yellow beads and complete rows 6 and 7. Alternate with 2 black and 2 yellow rows until you have 3 yellow stripes (rows 8 to 15) on the bee's body. Add 4 more black rows (rows 16 to 19). Begin to pull the top basic and bottom wires closer together, and add 3 more rows (rows 20 to 22). With nylon jaw-nose pliers, wrap the wire tightly around the bottom loop for about ⅓ inch, then clip it. This little twisted wire will be the bee's stinger.

2 Make 2 wings. Pattern: With the crystal beads, push the beads up to within 2 inches of the knot and make a 4-bead loop. Add 3 wraparound loops, leave 1½ inches of bare wire and clip from the spool. Twist the bare wires tightly together.

3 Twist together the stems of the 2 wings. Place the wire that is holding both of the wings into the bee's body at the first yellow stripe. Push the wire through the body until it protrudes out the end of the bee. Twist this wire once or twice around the stinger to secure.

4 With your fingers, mold the body of the bee into a curved cylinder and adjust the wings.

5 Attach the bee to one of the backyard flowers with a 5-inch length of gold assembly wire.

DESIGN TIP

Fill a crystal vase with pretty marbles and insert the flowers so their shiny stems are peeking out above them.

NEW TECHNIQUE

DOME

1 The dome (also called the beehive) technique is a popular method to make centers of blossoms. It's similar to the basic frame technique, but rather than working on a flat frame, you bend the top basic and bottom loop anywhere from 45° to 90° toward the bottom and work downward. The beaded rows on the side of the basic row will remain the same length or even decrease in size rather than increase. You can adjust the dome or beehive to achieve a variety of shapes. (See photo 2.)

2 You'll end the dome shape at the top basic instead of the bottom loop. This will give you 2 end wires. Twist together the basic wire and the ending wire and clip them.

PHOTO 2. THE DOME TECHNIQUE IS A MODIFIED BASIC FRAME.

Flowering Dogwood

A simple branch of flowering dogwood captures the essence of Southern charm. Shading brings an exquisite touch of realism to the petals—it's a technique you'll want to use on many other flowers.

Basic Techniques

Basic Frame (BF)
Continuous Loops (CL)

Special Techniques

Flossing the Stem
Split Loop

New Technique

Shading

Dogwood Blossom

4 petals with notched ends
2 leaves
1 inner center
1 outer center
1 calyx.

What You Need for 1 Dogwood Branch with 8 Blossoms

3 hanks	12/0 pink beads for petals
3 hanks	12/0 white beads for petals
1 hank	11/0 green beads for leaves, outer center, and calyx
2 strands	11/0 lighter green beads for inner center
1 spool	28-gauge white wire or 30-gauge white paddle wire for petals
1 spool	26-gauge green wire for leaves and center units
3 skeins	green silk or embroidery floss
1 piece	Wire coat hanger or other similar wire for the main branch, wrapped with brown floral tape
4 pieces	18-gauge stem wire for secondary branches, cut to varying shorter lengths, each wrapped in brown floral tape

Brown floral tape
Basic Flower-Making Kit

Making the Parts of the Dogwood Blossom

NOTE: These petals are tricky and require concentration. You'll be using a special technique (see the split loop in the Butterfly-Kissed Geranium project on page 61) as well as a new technique-shading-at the same time. Keep track of your colors and your rows!

1 Make 4 petals for each blossom. Pattern: With the pink beads, make a 6-bead BF, RT, RB, 8 rows, split the bottom loop and add 1 double row on each side, finish the 13th row at the bottom on the right side. Begin to shade the petal at the beginning of row 6. Use figures 1 through 5 as your pattern. It's not necessary to count the beads or to be exact.

2 After you finish row 8, split the bottom loop in the middle.

3 Bring the beaded wire from the basic wire to the right split loop and wrap it completely around the wire. (See figure 3.)

4 Take the beaded wire back up the right side to the top and wrap it around the basic wire. You have completed rows 9 and 10. Remember to shade your rows!

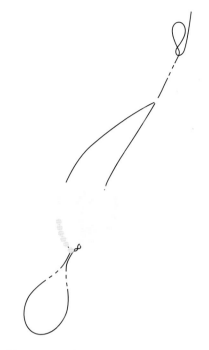

FIGURE 1. ADD PINK BEADS AT THE BEGINNING OF ROW 6.

FIGURE 2. YOU'VE COMPLETED 8 ROWS OF THE PETAL.

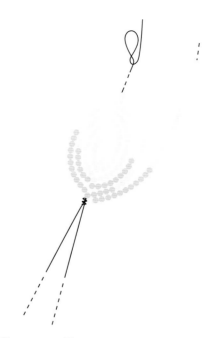

PHOTO 1. BEND THE WIRES FROM THE
SPLIT LOOP TO THE BACK.

5 With the front facing you, take
the beaded wire down the left
side and wrap around the left split
loop. (See figure 4.)

6 Bring the beaded wire back to
the basic wire and wrap. This
completes rows 11 and 12. Bring
the beaded wire down the right
side for row 13 and twist the spool
wire onto the right split loop.
Unlike the geranium that also uses

the split loop technique, it's the
top basic wire of the dogwood, not
the loop, that becomes the stem of
this petal. Clip each of the split
loops to ⅛ inch and bend the
wires to the back. (See photo 1
and figure 5.)

7 Make 1 inner center for each
blossom. Pattern: 5 CL with
10 beads each. Leave 2 inches of
bare wire on each end.

8 Make 1 outer center for each
blossom. Pattern: 7 CL with
13 beads each. Leave 2 inches of
bare wire on each end.

9 Make 1 calyx for each blossom.
Pattern: 5 CL with 12 beads
each. Leave 2 inches of bare wire
on each end.

10 Make 2 or 3 leaves for each
blossom. Pattern: 8-bead BF,
PT, RB, 5 rows, reduce to 1 wire.

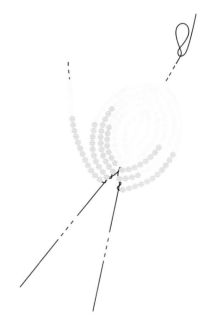

FIGURE 4. ROWS 11 AND 12 ARE ADDED
TO THE LEFT SIDE OF THE PETAL.

ASSEMBLING THE DOGWOOD BRANCH

1 Make the stem of each blossom by wrapping the outer center around the inner center and tightly twisting together the wires.

2 Attach the petals with the wire side facing down.

3 Add the calyx.

4 Wrap the blossom stems with brown floral tape for about 3½ inches.

5 Floss the stems for 2½ or 3 inches under the base of the blossom (see the flossing instructions in the Loving Roses project on page 91).

6 Attach a blossom to the main stem at the point where the flossing on the blossom ends. Wrap with brown floral tape. With the floral tape, attach 1 or 2 leaves to the main stem about 2 inches down from the blossom. In the same way, make 4 secondary branches by adding 1 or 2 blossoms and some leaves to the branch. Attach the secondary branches to the main stem with brown floral tape. You may want to add an extra branch or two that has only leaves as a graceful finishing note.

7 After you have assembled the branch, bend the stems a bit to make them look like a branch. Rub the branches with a little clear-drying glue. This will hold the floral tape in place and also give the branch a nice finish.

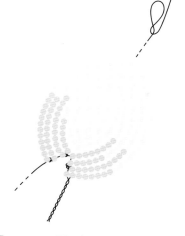

FIGURE 5. YOU'VE COMPLETED THE DOGWOOD PETAL.

DESIGN TIP

Instead of using pink shading, stay neutral. Close to the notch, shade the white petals with taupe or beige beads. Lovely, lovely!

NEW TECHNIQUE

SHADING

Shading allows you to blend colors within a flower part to show a natural gradation of color. Although it's time consuming, it creates rich and amazing-looking flowers. The directions below are specific to the dogwood, but the technique is easily transferable to other types of flowers.

1 Complete 5 rows on the dogwood with the pink beads, then estimate the amount of bare wire you'll need to complete the petal, add 6 inches, and clip the wire from the spool. Depending on the size of bead you're using, this may vary. For size 12 beads, you'll need about 24 inches.

2 To start row 6, add about ¼ or ⅜ inch of pink beads to go partially up the side.(See figure 1 on page 81.)

3 Add white beads that will complete row 6 and wrap around the top basic wire.

4 Add white beads to begin row 7 and pink beads to finish the row.

5 You'll need pink beads to begin row 8, and it's fine to put them on the wire at the same time. Finish row 8 with white beads.

6 Continue until 13 rows are complete. You don't have to count the number of beads, and you don't want each petal to look exactly like the others. Sometimes I start the shading on row 6 or row 8 to provide more variety and a realistic look.

Gold & White Orchid

*T*he Phalaenopsis orchid revels in its solitary elegance. Gold 2-cut size 12/0 beads add a gleam of luxury to the five snow-white blossoms. You'll use a new technique—the split basic—on the throat of the blossom, allowing you to put several components on one wire.

Basic Technique

Basic Frame (BF)

Special Techniques

Beading the Stem
Flossing the Stem
Lacing

New Technique

Split Basic

Orchid

5 blossoms, each with 2 wide and 3 narrow petals, and a throat with 2 petals (1 front and 1 back)
5 leaves

What You Need for 1 Orchid

3 hanks	11/0 or 12/0 white crystal beads for blossoms
2 hanks	11/0 green beads for leaves
1 hank	13/0 gold beads for throat petals
1 hank	11/0 brown beads to cover chopstick or other support
1 spool	24-gauge white wire (26-gauge white paddle wire will also work) for petals
1 spool	24-gauge green wire for leaves
1 spool	26-gauge gold wire for throat petals and to wrap chopstick
1 spool	30 to 34-gauge green lacing wire
10 pieces	18-gauge stem wire for blossom and leaf stems, cut into 4-inch lengths, wrapped in floral tape
1 piece	Wire coat hanger or similar wire for the stem, cut to 15 inches
2 skeins	green silk floss or embroidery floss

1 chopstick (or dowel) cut to 12 inches
Floral clay
Small bowl or planter at least 4 inches deep
Dried floral moss
Basic Flower-Making Kit

Making the Parts of the Orchid

1. Make 15 narrow petals (3 for each blossom). Pattern: 12-bead BF, RT, RB, 13 rows, reduce to 1 wire.

2. Make 10 wide petals (2 for each blossom). Pattern: 3-bead BF, RT, PB, 15 rows, reduce to 1 wire.

3. Make 5 throat front petals (1 for each blossom). Pattern: 20-bead BF, RT, RB, 5 rows, reduce to 1 wire.

4. See the instructions for the split basic technique on page 86. Make 5 throat back petals (1 for each blossom). Pattern: Using the split basic technique, make a 6-bead BF, PT, RB, 9 rows. Include 8 beads in the loop and make two 4-bead BF, RT, RB, 9 rows. Leave 2 inches of bare wire for the stem.

5. Make 5 leaves. Pattern: 2½-inch-bead BF, RT, RB, 5 rows, reduce to 2 wires and twist together the wires. Lace if necessary (see lacing instructions in the Three Cheery Spring Bulbs project on page 54).

Photo 1. The orchid throat contains a front and a back petal.

Assembling the Orchid

1. Make the throat unit. Place the front throat petal on the front side of the back throat petal between the two 4-bead BFs. Twist together the 2 wires. Bend the front petal out to a 90° angle, and then curl or roll it into a circle. (See photo 1.)

2. Unlike other flowers, the petals of the orchid aren't placed evenly around the stem. Instead, the 3 narrow petals are attached to the stem first with the 1st and 3rd petals opposite each other and the 2nd petal in between them. The 2 wider petals are placed in between the narrow petals. Attach the petals to 1 of the 4-inch wrapped stem wires.

3. Add the throat at the blossom base where all of the petals come together with the curled petal in the front. With your finger, gently cup the 3 sides of the throat.

4. Floss the stem for 2 inches. (See flossing instructions in the Loving Roses project on page 91.)

5 Repeat steps 1 through 4 for each of the blossoms.

6 With floss, attach each blossom on the main coat hanger stem, 3 blossoms on top and 2 on the bottom. Floss the stem to within the last 2 inches of the bottom of the stem.

7 With the chopstick, make the post to secure the orchid in the planter. Cover the chopstick with floral tape and then bead it with the brown beads (see beading the stem instructions in the Three Cheery Spring Bulbs project on page 53).

8 Work the floral clay with your hands to soften it, and press it into the bowl of the planter. Push the beaded chopstick post into the floral clay, and then insert the orchid stem as far as you can.

9 With about 4 inches of brown beaded wire, make 2 "twisties" to hold the orchid to the post.

10 Add moss around the base of the orchid.

11 Add a 4-inch stem to the base of each leaf and wrap with floral tape. Plant the leaves in the clay at the base of the stem around the back of the orchid.

12 Gently bend the orchid to give it a natural curve.

DESIGN TIP

Orchid blossoms look wonderful in wedding bouquets, especially if you shade their petals. See shading instructions in the Flowering Dogwood project on page 83.

NEW TECHNIQUE

SPLIT BASIC

For certain flowers (such as the orchid, the morning glory leaf, and the snapdragon), it's important to minimize the number of wires to reduce bulk. The split basic technique allows you to create several components of a flower with a small amount of wire. For example, with 1 wire and 1 frame, you can make the equivalent of 3 basic frame petals. Prepare the basic row as usual. However, when you make the bottom loop, thread enough beads for 2 more basic frames. When you finish, the single spool wire acts as the stem or anchor.

Here's how to use the split basic to make the back petal for the throat of the orchid.

1 Push 6 gold beads up to within 2 inches of the knot as you normally would.

2 When you form the bottom loop, use 5 inches of wire and push 8 beads from the spool inside the loop before making the bottom loop twist. (See figure 1.)

3 Work on the 6-bead BF and complete 9 rows as you normally would.

4 Push 4 beads on either side of the loop. Cut the loop in the middle and knot each end to keep the beads from slipping off.

5 Wrap the spool wire tightly for ⅛ inch on one of the sides close to the twist to create a new BF from which to work. (See figure 2.)

6 Push down the 4 beads on this side to the new twist and treat it as a new BF. Complete 9 rows, ending at the bottom of the frame that used to be the bottom loop.

7 Bring the spool wire to the other split loop and wrap the wire around the base.

8 Slip the 4 beads away from the base and with the spool wire wrap the loop wire tightly for about ⅛ inch.

9 Treat this wire as the beginning of a new BF and complete the 9 rows around the basic 4 beads. Finish at the bottom of the frame.

10 Wrap the spool wire around twice, leave 2 inches for the stem, and then cut. (See figure 3.)

11 Clip the tops of each of the 3 "basic" wires to ¾ inch and bend them to the backside of the petal.

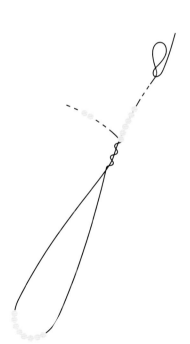

FIGURE 1. INCLUDE 8 BEADS IN THE BOTTOM LOOP.

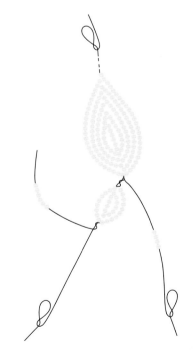

FIGURE 2. AFTER THE BOTTOM LOOP IS SPLIT, EACH SIDE IS TREATED AS A BASIC ROW AND A NEW FRAME IS BUILT.

FIGURE 3. HERE IS THE COMPLETED BACK PETAL.

Loving Roses

W hat could be a more convincing promise of everlasting love than two beautiful roses entwining? Each rose spray includes a fully opened rose with a smaller bloom and a bud. The petals of the open rose are outlined in a slightly different shade, adding richness and dimension. Flossing the stem with silk thread adds an elegant finish.

Basic Technique

Basic Frame (BF)

Special Techniques

Outlining
Reverse Basic

New Technique

Flossing the Stem

Rose Spray

Large open rose with 2 small,
  5 medium, and 5 large petals
Small blossom with 2 small and
  2 medium petals
Bud with 4 large petals
10 leaves
15 sepals, 5 for each flower

WHAT YOU NEED FOR 1 ROSE SPRAY

3 hanks	9/0 beads (Color A) for petals
1 hank	9/0 beads (Color B, slightly deeper shade) for outlining
3 hanks	9/0 green beads for leaves and sepals
2 spools	24-gauge colored wire for petals
1 spool	24-gauge green wire for leaves and sepals
1 spool	30 to 34-gauge assembly wire
2 pieces	18-gauge stem wire for the main stem, wrapped in floral tape
3 pieces	18-gauge wire as secondary stems for the blossom, bud, and leaves, cut in different lengths, wrapped in floral tape
Basic Flower-Making Kit	

MAKING THE ROSE SPRAY

1 In steps 2 through 5, you'll make the rose petals, beading most of the rows with the color A beads. Then you'll use the color B beads to outline the last rows in a different color. (See outlining instructions in the Anemone Accessory project on page 60.)

2 Make 4 small petals, 2 each for the open rose and the small blossom. Pattern: 5-bead BF, RT, RB, 15 rows, reduce to 1 wire. Outline the last 2 rows with color B.

3 Make 7 medium petals, 5 for the open rose, and 2 for the small blossom. Pattern: 5-bead BF, RT, RB, 19 rows, reduce to 1 wire. Outline the last 4 rows with color B.

4 Make 9 large petals, 5 for the open rose and 4 for the bud. Pattern: 5-bead BF, RT, RB, 21 rows, reduce to 1 wire. Outline the last 4 rows with color B.

5 Make 1 large petal for the bud, using the reverse basic technique (see instructions in the Floating Gardenia project on page 47). Pattern: 5-bead BF, RT, RB, reverse basic, 21 rows, reduce to 1 wire. Outline the last 4 rows with color B.

4 Push the 4 petals open.

5 Make the bud. Take 3 large petals, with the wire side facing in, and bend the sides of the petals slightly to the center. With the wire side facing in, attach the petals to the top of a secondary stem.

6 With the bottom wire facing in, attach the large petal made with the reverse basic technique. Bend the top of this petal slightly over the back to cover the wire.

7 Attach the sepals with the wire side facing in toward the bud. Sepals protect the bud and so these should be pointed upward covering the bottom of the petals.

8 Floss from the top of the stem, adding 2 leaves about 2 inches down and another leaf 2 inches below that. Floss for another 3 inches. Wrap with floral tape to secure the floss endings.

9 Make a leaf stem. Add a small leaf to the top of another secondary stem wire. Floss from the top of the stem down a few inches and add 2 more leaves. Floss at least another 3 inches, and then wrap the bottom of the floss with floral tape to secure it.

10 Make the large rose. Take 2 small petals, wire side facing in, and attach them to the top of the main stem wire. With the wire side facing out, add the 5 medium petals. In similar manner, add the 5 large petals. Finally, add the sepals with the wire side facing out. Bend the sepals downward.

6 Make 5 small leaves. Pattern: 5-bead BF, PT, RB, 13 rows, reduce to 2 wires and twist together the wires.

7 Make 2 medium leaves. Pattern: 5-bead BF, RT, RB, 17 rows, reduce to 2 wires and twist.

8 Make 2 large leaves. Pattern: 5-bead BF, RT, RB, 21 rows, reduce to 2 wires and twist.

9 Make 15 sepals, 5 each for the large and small roses and 5 for the rosebud. Pattern: 10-bead BF, PT, PB, 5 rows, reduce to 1 wire.

ASSEMBLING THE ROSE SPRAY

1 Make the small blossom. Take 1 medium petal, wire side facing out, and, attach it to the top of a secondary stem. Attach a large petal next to it, followed by a medium petal, and then another large petal.

2 Attach the sepals.

3 Floss from the top of the stem to the bottom about 1½ inches and wrap with floral tape to secure the floss endings (see flossing instructions on opposite page).

PHOTO 1. SEPARATE THE STRANDS OF THE FLOSS.

PHOTO 1. SEPARATE THE STRANDS OF THE FLOSS.

PHOTO 2. WRAP THE FLOSS AROUND THE STEM.

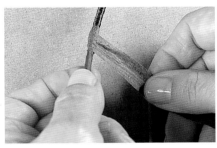

PHOTO 3. SECURE THE FLOSS WITH FLORAL TAPE.

11 After you've attached all of the petals, use matching 30-gauge wire to weave in and out of the rows on the bottom layer of petals to secure them. It is not necessary to weave or sew in and out of every row. Take care not to allow the wire to show on the front of the blossom.

12 Begin to floss the stem of the open rose. About 1 inch under the sepals, add 2 leaves. Continue to floss another 3 inches or so. Add the secondary stem wire with the bud so that the bud is about 2 inches higher than the rose. Floss 1/2 inch.

13 Add the secondary stem wire with the 3 leaves so that the leaves are slightly above the rose. Floss a few more inches. Add the small rose. Floss 1 inch or so and add 2 leaves, then floss another 2 inches. Finish by wrapping the bottom of the flossed area with 1/2 to 1 inch of floral tape.

DESIGN TIP

To make a stunning opening-night arm bouquet, tie several rose sprays together with wide ribbon. Add baby's breath (see instructions in the Beaded Bridal Bouquet project on page 98) and fern (see instructions in the Summer Perennial project on page 78).

NEW TECHNIQUE

FLOSSING THE STEM

1 Divide the skein of embroidery or silk floss in half. Hold all the strands together and smooth them with your fingers. (See photo 1.)

2 Press 1 inch of the floss lengthwise on the stem as close as possible to the flower base, and wrap the stem with the remaining floss that hangs down the stem. (This technique is similar to beading the stem in the Three Cheery Spring Bulbs project on page 53, just with much thinner material. (See photo 2.)

3 Floss about 8 inches down the stem. Keep the floss as smooth as possible by straightening it with your fingers. Secure the floss with a drop of clear-drying glue. When you are finished, wrap 1 inch of floral tape around the bottom of the stem to further secure the floss. (See photo 3.)

4 If you run out of floss, simply tack the bottom of the floss with a little glue or floral tape and begin with a new piece.

Beaded Bridal Bouquet & Boutonnière

The lucky bride can keep her beaded bouquet forever, even passing it on to her daughter for her special day. It sparkles in a happy color combination: lace-white carnations, blue freesias, pink roses, and a kiss of red clover. A new technique—loop-back leaves—adds unique leaves to the carnation when needed for another project.

Basic Techniques

Basic Frame (BF)
Continuous Crossover Loops (CCL)
Continuous Loops (CL)

Special Techniques

Beading the Stem
Flossing the Stem
Lacing
Reverse Basic
Split Basic

New Technique

Loop-Back Leaves

Wedding Bouquet

5 carnations (no leaves)
10 clovers (with leaves)
5 freesias (1 stem with 1 blossom
   and 2 buds; 2 stems with
   1 blossom and 1 bud; 2 stems
   with 1 blossom only)
5 roses (no leaves)

NOTES

Though not absolutely necessary, you may want to finish the stems of the flowers by flossing them with silk thread or beading them. See flossing instructions in the Loving Roses project on page 91 and beading the stem instructions in Three Cheery Spring Bulbs on page 53.

The leaves in this bouquet are limited to those on the clovers. When you want to add leaves for the carnation, the freesia, or the roses, see the instructions on page 99.

Carnation

14 petal sections
1 calyx

WHAT YOU NEED FOR
1 CARNATION

1 hank	11/0 or 12/0 colored beads for petals (I used white)
1 hank	11/0 green beads for calyx
1 spool	24-gauge colored wire for beads
1 spool	24-gauge green wire for calyx
2 pieces	18-gauge stem wires, wrapped with floral tape.

Basic Flower-Making Kit

MAKING THE PARTS OF THE CARNATION

1 Make 8 small petal sections. Pattern: Make 5 CL with 1½ inches of beads each. Leave 2 inches of bare wire on each side.

2 Make 6 large petal sections. Pattern: Make 7 CL with 2 inches of beads each. Leave 2 inches of bare wire on each side. Twist the top half of each loop.

3 Make 1 calyx. Pattern: Make 10 CL with 2 1/2 inches of beads each. Leave 2 inches of bare wire on each side. With your fingers, squeeze together the sides of the loops. Wrap assembly wire around the top ½ inch of the first loop. Pull the wire tight to secure it, and wrap under and around the top ½ inch of the next beaded loop. Again, gently pull the wire tight to bring the beaded loops together. Continue to the end. Wrap the wire around the last beaded loop twice to secure it. One side of the calyx will have more wire showing than the other—this is the back side. The side with the wire showing is the inside of the calyx. Bend each tip over the wire side of the calyx. (See photo 1.)

PHOTO 1. BEND THE TIPS OF THE LOOPS TO FORM THE CALYX.

Assembling the Carnation

1 Attach the 8 small petal sections to a wrapped stem.

2 Attach the 6 large petal sections around the 8 small ones.

3 Wrap the calyx around the base of the carnation blossom with the bent tips facing outward. Connect the 1st and 10th loops of the calyx together at the top and bottom. The blossom will look like it's growing out of the calyx. (See photo 2.)

Photo 2. Wrap the calyx around the stem.

Clover

(See instructions in the Tussie Mussie with Red Clover project on page 43.)
10 blossoms
40 leaves

Freesia

5 petals
1 center
2 large buds
1 small bud

What You Need for 1 Freesia

1 hank	11/0 or 12/0 blue, pink, or purple beads for petals
1 hank	11/0 or 12/0 slightly lighter color for blossom center and buds
1 spool	24-gauge colored wire for petals
1 spool	26-gauge green wire for calyx
1 piece	18-gauge stem wire for main stem, wrapped with floral tape
1 piece	18-guage stem wire, cut to 4 inches for buds, wrapped with floral tape

Basic Flower-Making Kit

MAKING THE PARTS OF THE FREESIA

1 Make 5 petals. Pattern: 3-bead BF, PT, PB, 7 rows, reduce to 1 wire.

2 Make 1 center. Pattern: 3-bead BF, RT, RB, 5 rows, reduce to 1 wire.

3 Make 2 large buds. (See the split basic technique in the Gold & White Orchid project on page 86.) Pattern: 3-bead BF, RT, RB, 7 rows. Place 6 beads in the basic loop and, using the split basic technique, complete two 3-bead BFs, RT, RB, 7 rows on each side of the loop. You'll have a total of 3 BFs, 1 on the top basic wire and 2 on the loop. With your fingers, fold the 3 petals toward each other so that the top of each is touching the top of the other 2. Wrap the stem of the bud with floral tape.

4 Make 1 small bud. Pattern: 3-bead BF, RT, RB, 5 rows. Place 6 beads in the basic loop and, using the split basic technique that you used for the 2 large buds, complete two 3-bead BFs, RT, RB, 5 rows on each side of the loop. You will have a total of 3 BFs, one on the top basic wire and 2 on the loop. With your fingers, fold the 3 petals toward each other so that the top of each is touching the top of the other 2. Wrap the stem of the bud with floral tape.

ASSEMBLING THE FREESIA

1 Attach the center unit to the top of the main stem.

2 Add the petals.

3 Add the small bud to the top of the 4-inch piece of stem wire. About 2 inches below it, add the larger bud.

4 With floral tape, attach the bud stem to the main stem so that the buds are about 1 or 2 inches above the blossom.

Note: Assemble the other freesia stems with different combinations of blossoms, and buds, both large and small.

Rose

12 petals
1 calyx

WHAT YOU NEED FOR 1 ROSE

2 hanks	9/0 colored beads for petals (I used pink)
1 hank	9/0 transparent green beads for calyx
1 spool	24-gauge wire for petals
1 spool	24-gauge wire for calyx
2 skeins	green silk thread or embroidery floss
2 pieces	18-gauge stem wires, wrapped with floral tape
1 spool	30 to 34-gauge lacing wire to match color of petals

Basic Flower-Making Kit

ASSEMBLING THE ROSE

1 With the wire side of the petals facing in, attach the 2 small petals with assembly wire to the top of the wrapped stem wires. Bend the petals with your fingers so that they nestle into one another.

2 Take each of the 2 medium petals and, with your thumb on the inside where the wire shows, gently press into the bottom of the petal to create a cupping effect. Attach the medium petals around the small petals.

3 Attach the large petals around the medium petals and with your fingers, curl the tips of the tops back. Notice that because the petals were made with the reverse basic technique, no wire shows on the bottom of the blossom. (See photo 3.)

4 To secure the blossom and to prevent the petals from falling to the outside, use a needle threaded with assembly wire to weave in and out of the outer row of petals. Take care not to allow the wire to show on the outside of the blossom. (See photo 4.)

5 Attach the calyx.

6 If you wish to floss the stem, do so according to the flossing technique n the Loving Roses project on page 91.

PHOTO 3. CURL THE OUTER PETAL TOPS.

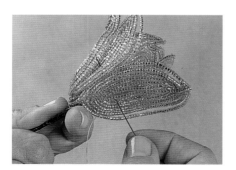

PHOTO 4. SEW ASSEMBLY WIRE IN AND OUT OF THE PETALS.

MAKING THE PARTS OF THE ROSE

1 Make 2 small petals. Pattern: 20-bead BF, RT, RB, 11 rows, reduce to 1 wire.

2 Make 2 medium petals. Pattern: 20-bead BF, RT, RB, 13 rows, reduce to 1 wire.

3 See the reverse basic technique in the Floating Gardenia project on page 47. Make 8 large petals. Pattern: 20-bead BF, RT, RB, reverse basic, 15 rows, reduce to 1 wire

4 Make 1 calyx. Pattern: Make 5 CCL beginning with 3 inches of beads for each loop. Leave 2 inches of bare wire on each side.

ASSEMBLING THE BRIDAL BOUQUET

Arrange the bouquet so that the flowers and colors are evenly distributed. Use the clovers and freesias to separate the carnations and roses. If there's not enough green, make a few more clover leaves and add them. Wrap together the stems of all the flowers with floral tape. This could take 1 or 2 yards of floral tape. Then wrap the stems with ribbon or use a bouquet sleeve, available from a crafts store, to cover the stem wires.

The Boutonnière

1 medium bud
1 leaf
Baby's breath

You can make the bridegroom's boutonnière out of any flower used in the bride's bouquet. For this particular one, use the pattern for the small blossom described in the Loving Roses project on page 90. Make the petals a little smaller by eliminating the last 2 rows on each petal. Make 1 or 2 blossoms; add a few leaves and some baby's breath. Attach the boutonnière to the lapel with a floral pin.

BABY'S BREATH

1 Baby's breath is a combination of simple loops and twisted bare wire. String 28-gauge wire with small white beads. Make a single loop with 5 to 7 beads and twist the wire tightly for an inch or two. Push the beads 2 inches away from the twist and then make another loop and twist. Push the beads out for a third time and make another loop. You can also leave an occasional bead or two in the twisted wire to add a little more interest.

FIGURE 1. BABY'S BREATH IS MADE BY PUSHING A FEW BEADS AWAY FROM THE END OF THE WIRE AND TWISTING THE WIRE TO FORM A STEM. AN OCCASIONAL BEAD IN THE WIRE ADDS INTEREST.

2 When you have 3 branches, twist the wire for a few inches, push the beads out a few inches, and make another branch. You can make baby's breath as full or as sparse as you wish. For the boutonniere, we used white 28-gauge wire. You can also use green or gold, depending on what effect you want to achieve. (See figure 1.)

MAKING LEAVES FOR THE FREESIA

1 Make the freesia leaves using the leaf pattern in the Desktop Marigolds project on page 113.

MAKING LEAVES FOR THE ROSE

1 Make the leaves using the leaf pattern in the Loving Roses project on page 90.

NEW TECHNIQUE

LOOP-BACK LEAVES

Loop-back leaves are similar to the basic frame leaves used in most of the projects in the book. They have 1 or more sets of double loops on each side of the frame which add interest. Here's how to make a loop-back leaf specifically for the carnation.

1 Make two 20-bead BFs, PT, RB, 9 rows.

2 When you have finished row 9, take the beaded wire up the left side and make a simple loop that sits on the left side of the basic row, slightly below the top of the leaf.

3 When you are finished, the beaded wire will be at the bottom loop. Wrap the bare wire around the bottom loop. On the right side of the basic frame, make a simple loop equal to the one on the left side. Again, the beaded wire will be at the bottom loop. (See figure 2.)

4 Back on the left side, make a 3rd loop that will sit alongside and slightly lower than the 1st one.

5 Repeat step 4 on the other side. (See figure 3.)

6 Slightly bend the tips of these loops. If necessary, lace across the rows of the BF rows and loops to secure the structure of the leaf.

FIGURE 2. A LOOP-BACK LEAF HAS SIMPLE LOOPS ON EITHER SIDE OF THE BASIC FRAME.

FIGURE 3. HERE'S THE COMPLETED LOOP-BACK LEAF WITH 2 DOUBLE LOOPS ON EITHER SIDE.

Striped Tiger Lily

The tiger lily is so stunning, it doesn't need anything but its own glorious self to grab all the attention. This version glows with yellow and orange beads, striped with golden brown. A cluster of stamens rises majestically out of its center.

Basic Technique

Basic Frame (BF)

Special Techniques

Beading the Stem
Lacing
Outlining

New Technique

Striping

Tiger Lily

6 petals
7 stamens
1 bud (made of 2 leaves)

What You Need for 1 Tiger Lily

1 hank	11/0 orange beads for petals
1 hank	11/0 brown/orange beads for petals
1 hank	11/0 green beads for bud and stem
1 hank	11/0 pale green or yellow beads for stamens
1 strand	11/0 brown beads for the top of the stamens
1 spool	24-gauge gold wire for petals
1 spool	24-gauge green wire for bud
1 spool	28-gauge gold wire for stamens
2 pieces	18-gauge stem wires, wrapped with floral tape
1 spool	30- to 34-gauge lacing wire to match petals

Basic Flower-Making Kit

Making the Parts of the Tiger Lily

1 Make 6 petals. Pattern: 1½-inch-bead BF, PT, PB, 17 rows, reduce to 1 wire. When putting the beads on the wire, add ½ inch or so of the brown beads every couple of inches. This will add color stripes to the petals and make them look realistic. Also outline the last 2 rows of each petal with the brown beads (see the outlining technique in the Anemone Accessory project on page 60). (See figure 1.)

2 Make 7 stamens. Pattern: String 2½ inches of pale green beads on 28-gauge wire. Add 15 brown beads. Make a loop with the brown beads. Wrap bare wire around the brown loop 2 times to secure the beads and clip close to the wire. On the other side, leave about 2 inches of bare wire and clip from the spool. (See figure 2.)

3 When you have finished all 7 stamens, push the beads of each up to the loop and tightly twist together all their bare wires.

4 Make 2 leaves to form the bud. Pattern: 1½-inch-bead BF, PT, PB, 11 rows, reduce to 1 wire. With their wire sides facing in, hold together the 2 leaves and twist the wires. Twist together the leaves to create a spiral.

Assembling the Tiger Lily

1 Place the group of stamens at the top of the wrapped stem wires so that the edge of beads is even with the top of the stem. Wrap and secure with assembly wire.

2 With assembly wire, add the petals 1 at a time underneath the stamens and evenly distributed around them.

3 Lace together the petals with matching wire to secure the blossom. (See instructions on page 54.)

4 Wrap the stem with floral tape to hide the wires.

5 Bead the stem (see instructions in the Three Cheery Spring Bulbs project on page 53). Add the bud at about 2 inches below the blossom.

6 Using the pattern for the daffodil leaf on page 49, make 3 or 4 leaves and attach them along the stem as you bead it.

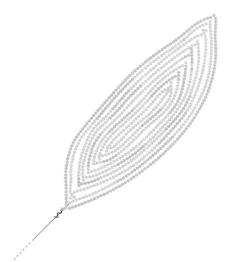

FIGURE 1. THE LILY PETAL HAS STRIPES OF A DARKER COLOR THROUGHOUT.

FIGURE 2. A LILY STAMEN IS A SINGLE LOOP WITH BEADS ON THE WIRE.

New Technique

Striping

Striping is a simple way to add color to a petal or a leaf. Like shading, you'll have to cut the wire from the spool. However, you don't have to add the beads row by row. Instead, you can add several inches of color A, then ½ inch or so of color B, several inches of color A, 1 inch of color B, and so on. The result is a remarkably realistic looking flower.

Design Tip

Greet Easter with a display of white lilies and magnificent yellow-gold stamens.

Victorian Parlor Basket

*T*his precious basket of morning glories, portulaca (moss rose), and violets would have been right at home in a Victorian parlor.

To create the unique petals of the morning glory, you'll make a frame of five spokes to hold the beaded wire. The portulaca uses continuous wraparound loops, and the violet, continuous crossover loops. The stem tops for all three flowers and all of the leaves are beaded in two ways—beading the top part of the stem and stringing larger beads directly onto the stem.

DESIGN BY ROBERTA TROEDER

WHAT YOU NEED FOR 5 MORNING GLORIES

1 hank	11/0 lavender beads for blossoms
1 hank	11/0 purple beads for blossoms
1 hank	11/0 green beads for leaves
1 tube	8/0 green for the stems of the morning glory and leaves
1 tube	11/0 yellow beads for stamens
1 spool	26-gauge purple or lavender wire for blossoms
1 spool	28-gauge green wire for leaves
1 spool	24-gauge silver wire for spokes
1 spool	30 to 34-gauge gold lacing wire for stamens
1 spool	22-gauge green wire for stems

Basic Flower-Making Kit

MAKING THE PARTS OF THE MORNING GLORY

1 Make the blossom. See the instructions below on making a spoke frame and make one with 5 pieces of 24-gauge wire cut to 6-inch lengths. Spread apart the spokes. Pull the beaded wire that is attached to the stem to the outside of the frame. Push 2 beads to the end of the wire and wrap bare wire around the first spoke. Push 2 beads to fill the next section (the area between the spokes) and wrap bare wire around the next spoke. Continue until you have wrapped all 5 spokes. Keep the row of beads as close to the center of the frame as you can. You have completed row 1.

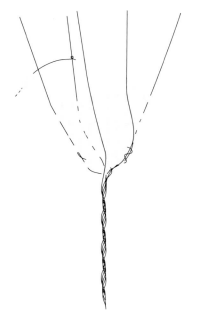

FIGURE 1. CREATE THE MORNING GLORY BY WRAPPING ROWS OF BEADS AROUND A SERIES OF SPOKES THAT ARE SHAPED LIKE A CONE.

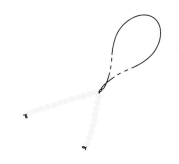

FIGURE 2. MAKE A DOUBLE STAMEN FOR THE MORNING GLORY BY TWISTING THE WIRE AND ADDING BEADS ON EACH END. COIL THE TIP OF THE WIRE TIGHTLY AROUND A PIN TO SECURE THE BEADS.

7 Make 3 leaves with 3 leaflets each. Pattern: Use the split basic technique (see instructions in the Gold & White Orchid project on pages 86-87) to make 3 leaflets on 1 frame and minimize the amount of wire. Make a 7-bead BF and include 14 beads in the BF loop. On the 7-bead BF, make a PT, RB, 7 rows. When you have finished the BF, split the bottom loop and knot each end to keep the beads from falling off. On each side of the split loop, make a 7-bead BF, RT, PB, 7 rows. When finished with the 3rd BF, twist the spool wire 2 times at the base of the 3 frames, leave 2 inches of bare wire and clip the wire from the spool. Make sure that the wire side of each leaf is on the same side. (See figure 3.)

2 Continue wrapping the beaded wire around the spokes for rows 2 through 10. Add 1 extra bead to each section every time you complete a row. At row 10, you should have 12 beads per section. As you wrap the spokes, keep the wires as close together as you can. (See figure 1.)

3 For row 11, you'll change colors and also bend the frame so there is a lip on the blossom. Add 2 beads per section (making it now 14 beads per row) and bend the spokes outward so that the extra wire and beads fit properly between the spokes.

4 Continue wrapping the beads around the spokes for rows 12 through 14, increasing 1 bead per section. Maintain the slight curve or bend on the edge. On row 14, you should have 17 beads per section.

At the end of row 14, wrap the bare spool wire around the spoke 3 times to secure it.

5 Trim the spoke wires to ¼ inch and bend them to the back.

6 Make 10 double stamens, 2 for each blossom. Thread about 12 inches of yellow beads onto 30-gauge wire. Clip any knot from the end of the wire. Coil the wire tightly around a needle or 22-gauge piece of wire a few times. This will make an attractive knot to keep the beads from falling off. Move ¾ inch of beads close to the coil. Directly under the beads, make a loop with 3 inches of bare wire and twist. Push ¾ inch of beads down to the twist and make another coil close to the beads. Clip the wire at the end of the coil. You will have 2 stamens coming off a single loop of bare wire. (See figure 2.)

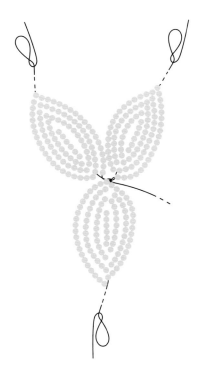

FIGURE 3. MAKE THE MORNING GLORY LEAVES WITH THE SPLIT BASIC TECHNIQUE.

ASSEMBLING THE MORNING GLORY

1 Insert a 9-inch piece of 22-gauge stem wire into the hole at the base of the blossom. Make a ½-inch open loop with the top of the wire, loop it over 1 of the spokes, and pull it down under the flower. The blossom now has a stem wire. Wrap the top 1 inch of the stem with floral tape to cover the loop and spoke wires.

2 Wrap the green beaded wire around the top of the floral tape to create a calyx (see the beading the stem instructions for the daffodil in the Three Cheery Spring Bulbs project on page 53). End by wrapping bare wire around the stem twice. Push the bare wire as close as you can to the beaded stem. Thread the 8/0 green beads onto the bare stem for about 7 inches. Wrap floral tape around the bottom of the stem to secure the beads.

3 To shape the flower, gently mold the sections between the spokes and press them in toward the center of the flower. This will make the outer edge look ruffled or star shaped.

4 Add a stem to each leaf by placing a 9-inch piece of 22-gauge wire around the middle leaflet. Loop the stem wire around the wire of the leaf to secure it. Wrap floral tape around the top 1 inch of the stem wire. Bead the wire as you did in step 1 for making the blossom.

5 Wrap the stem around a dowel or pencil 2 or 3 times. This will give it a slight curl, making it look as if it were just cut off the vine.

Portulaca

10 blossoms (each with 1 small unit and 1 large unit)
10 leaves

WHAT YOU NEED FOR 10 PORTULACAS

1 hank	11/0 light peach	for blossoms
1 hank	11/0 medium peach	for blossoms
1 hank	11/0 green beads	for leaves
1 tube	8/0 green beads	for stems of blossom
11 beads	3mm copper fire-polished,	for flower center
1 spool	26-gauge colored wire	for petals
1 spool	24-gauge green wire	for leaves
10 pieces	22-gauge green wire	for blossom stems, to 3 inches

Basic Flower-Making Kit

MAKING THE PARTS OF THE PORTULACA

The portulaca blossom is made with 2 units of continuous wrap-around loops, each formed into a circle. The smaller unit is then placed on top of the larger one. Add variety to the flowers by changing the colors. Make some of the blossoms a single color of light or medium peach, and make others with 1 unit of light peach and the other with the darker color.

1 Make the small blossom unit. Pattern: Make 5 CWL, 3 loops each, beginning with a 3-bead loop. Leave 3 inches of bare wire on each side. Make a circle with the strip of CWL. Add a 3 mm fire-polished bead to 1 of the end wires and wrap it across the front of the petals for the center. Bring the wire through 2 of the loops to the underside of the loops.

FIGURE 4. THE PORTULACA LEAF IS A
SERIES OF TWISTED
CONTINUOUS LOOPS.

2 Make the large blossom unit.
Pattern: Make 5 CWL, 3 loops
each, beginning with a 5-bead
loop. Leave 3 inches of bare wire
on each side.

3 Make 10 leaves. Pattern: Start
with a 12-bead loop very close
to the end of the spool wire. Clip
any excess wire from the loop. Slide
3 beads from the spool wire up
against the loop, starting the stem.
Make a 12-bead loop on 1 side of
the stem. Add 3 beads and then
make another 12-bead loop, this
time on the other side of the stem.
Continue until you have 6 loops on
each side. Leave 3 inches of bare
wire and clip from the spool. Finish
by giving each loop a ½ -inch twist.
(See figure 4.)

ASSEMBLING THE PORTULACA

1 Put the small blossom unit on
top of the large blossom unit.
With assembly wire, attach both to
1 of the 3-inch 22-gauge wire stems.
Wrap beaded wire around the top
of the stem under the blossom for
about ½ to ¾ inch. Wrap bare
wire around the stem to secure it,
and clip the wire from the spool.
Thread about 1½ to 2 inches of
size 8/0 on the stem and press it
close to the beaded wire. Wrap the
bottom of the stem with floral tape
to secure the beads.

2 Divide the 10 portulacas into
2 bunches. Make sure that there
are a variety of stem lengths in each
group. Wrap floral tape around
the bottom of the flower stems to
secure the beads. With floral tape,
attach 5 leaves around each bunch.

Violet

10 blossoms
5 leaves (2 large, 3 small)

WHAT YOU NEED FOR
10 VIOLETS

1 hank	11/0 purple beads for blossoms
1 hank	11/0 green beads for leaves
1 strand	11/0 yellow beads for center
1 tube	8/0 green beads for stems
1 spool	26-gauge colored wire for blossoms
1 spool	24-gauge green wire for leaves
10 pieces	22-gauge wire for stems, cut to varying 5 to 6-inch lengths

MAKING THE PARTS OF THE VIOLET

1 Make 10 blossoms. Pattern: Make 5 CCL, beginning with a 1-inch loop. Leave 5 inches of bare wire on each side. Add 3 yellow beads to an end wire and bring it between 2 petals to the front of the flower for a center. Take the bare wire between 2 opposite petals and twist the wire 3 times directly under the blossom. You will have 2 loose wires for the stem.

2 Make 2 large leaves. Pattern: 6-bead BF, PT, RB, 15 rows, reduce to 1 wire about 3 inches long.

3 Make 3 small leaves. Pattern: 6-bead BF, PT, RB, 13 rows, reduce to 1 wire about 3 inches long.

ASSEMBLING THE VIOLET

1 Bead the stems of the flowers. Place 1½ to 2¼ inches of green 8/0 beads on the stem wires of each of the flowers. Wrap floral tape around the bottom ½ inch of the stem wire to secure the beads. (See figure 5.)

2 Bead the stems of the leaves. Place 1½ to 2 inches of green 11/0 beads on each stem wire for the leaves. Wrap floral tape around the bottom ½ inch of the stems and then tape together the stems for all 5 leaves.

FIGURE 5. THE VIOLET HAS 5 CCLs.

3 Make a cluster of the 10 violets. Tape together the 2 tallest flowers; add each of the other flowers, 1 at a time, around the center flowers. Add the leaves in the same manner. Adjust the height of the stems if necessary to create an attractive cluster.

Parlor Basket

WHAT YOU NEED FOR 1 BASKET

2 hanks	11/0 gold beads
8 pieces	22-gauge gold wire for spikes, cut to 9 inches
1 spool	24-gauge gold wire

1 small polystyrene coffee cup to fit inside the basket
Floral clay
Dried moss
Basic Flower-Making Kit

MAKING THE BASKET

1 Hold together all the wire pieces and twist them tightly for 1½ inches. Spread out the spokes as in an opened umbrella.

2 Put at least 1½ hanks of gold beads on the 24-gauge wire. Wrap 1 inch of the bare spool wire around the twisted spoke wires. Bring the spool wire up between 2 spokes.

3 Row 1. Weave 1 bead between 2 spokes. Bring the wire over the next spoke, under it, and then over it again (for 1 complete loop). Repeat this process of going around the spokes until there is 1 bead alternating with each spoke.

4 Row 2. Place 2 beads between spokes as you continue wrapping the wire around each spoke.

5 Rows 3 to 15. Continue weaving the beads between spokes and wrapping the wire around each spoke. Increase the number of beads between spokes until you reach 15. Occasionally, you may have to put 1 more or 1 less bead between spokes. In the following

THE COMPLETED BASKET SHOWS THE 8 SPOKES AND THE INCREASING NUMBER OF BEADS IN THE ROWS BETWEEN THEM.

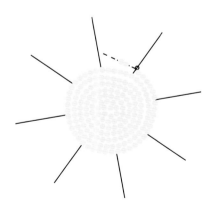

FIGURE 6. THE BASKET IS CREATED BY WRAPPING ROWS OF BEADS AROUND A SERIES OF SPOKES.

row, you'd make up for the added or deleted bead, returning to the right number of beads. Make sure you keep the piece flat with the twisted wires perpendicular to your work. Keep the spokes straight. (See figure 6.)

6 At the end of 15 rows, trim the twisted spoke wires that you made in step 1 to 1 inch and wrap them with floral tape.

7 Rows 16 to 26. Turn the spokes up and perpendicular to the original circle. Place 16 beads in each section and wrap each spoke 1 complete turn.

8 Rows 27 to 30. Increase 1 bead each row. At the end of 30 rows, you will have 19 beads per section.

9 Rows 31 to 32. Increase to 20 beads and continue wrapping.

10 Rows 33 to 34. Increase to 21 beads and continue wrapping.

11 Rows 35 to 37. Increase 1 bead each row and continue wrapping. At the end of row 37, you'll have 24 beads per section.

12 Row 38. Begin to form the lip of the basket. Increase the number of beads per section to 25. As you work, gradually bend the

spokes perpendicular to the basket and parallel to the bottom. At this point, to hide the wires, reverse the way you are wrapping the spokes. Rather than going over-under-over the wire, you will want to go under-over-under. This is similar to the reverse basic technique in the Floating Gardenia project on page 45.

13 Rows 39 to 45. Increase 1 bead per row. At the end of 45 rows, you'll have 32 beads per section.

14 Wrap the bare spool wire tightly around the spoke 3 times. Clip the wire from the spool. Trim the spoke wires to 3/8 inch and bend them back against the underside.

MAKING THE BASKET HANDLE

1 Decide what length you want your handle to be, then cut 2 pieces of 24-gauge wire that are 2 inches longer. Attach the 2 wires at a spoke 2 rows below the lip of the basket. Put enough beads on each wire to reach the opposite spoke. Twist together the 2 beaded wires and attach them on the other side. Trim the wires.

ASSEMBLING THE BASKET OF FLOWERS

1 Trim the coffee cup to fit inside the basket, to line and protect it. Soften floral clay with your hands, spread it on the bottom of the cup, and place it in the basket.

2 Plant your flowers and leaves. Arrange them like you would "real" flowers. Don't be afraid to shorten or even lengthen stems. Add dried moss to cover the clay.

DESIGN TIP

These tiny flowers are so delightful that any one of them, or a combination of all three, would make a sweet brooch or hair accessory. (See the Anemone Accessory project on page 59 and the Classic Poppy Pin on page 33.)

NEW TECHNIQUE

SPOKE FRAME

Occasionally you'll come across a flower with which none of the basic techniques seem to work, and you have to figure out new solutions. An easy fix for the morning glory was to create a series of spokes that could be wrapped to create the basketlike shape. Spokes are also used in the holly leaf on page 118 and could be used in other flowers that you choose. Note that the basket that holds the flowers in this project is beaded. It uses this same technique; instead of 5 spokes and 14 rows of beads, it has 8 spokes and 45 rows of beads.

Here's how to set up a frame of spokes.

1 Take 5 (or whatever number is specified in the pattern) pieces of 24-gauge wire cut to 6 inches and hold them together so the ends are even.

2 With jaw-nose or flat-nose pliers, twist together at least 1 inch of the gathered wires.

3 Wrap the spool wire around this stem and push it up to the side of 1 of the spokes. Separate the spokes as evenly as you can. You are ready to start beading the rows.

Snapdragon Stalks

A snapdragon display creates a vertical color splash in any location. This pattern, based on one by beaded flower legend Virginia Nathanson, is the most complicated flower project in this book—and what a sense of accomplishment you'll have when you finish it! It uses two techniques to form its unique petal formation: a modified basic frame to form the back petal, and the split basic technique for the front petal. Squiggly stamens draw attention to the blossoms.

Basic Technique

Continuous Loops (CL)
Basic Frame (BF)

Special Techniques

Split Basic

Snapdragon Stalk

7 buds, 3 small and 4 large
9 blossoms, with 18 petals
   (9 small front and 9 large back)
16 leaves, 8 small and 8 large
9 calyxes

What You Need for 1 Stalk of Snapdragons

3 hanks	11/0 or 12/0 beads for blossoms
2 hanks	11/0 green beads for leaves
1 hank	11/0 pale green beads for stamens
1 spool	26-gauge gold wire for blossoms
1 spool	26-gauge green wire for leaves, stamens, and calyxes
2 pieces	18-gauge stem wire, wrapped with floral tape
9 pieces	26-gauge gold wire, cut to 7-inch lengths
Basic Flower-Making Kit	

Making the Parts of the Snapdragon

1 Make 3 small buds. Pattern: On 1 wire, make 3 CL with 15 beads, 1 CL with 20 beads, and 3 CL with 15 beads. Leave 2 inches of bare wire on each side. Bring together the 2 ends and twist tightly. Bend the middle CL down over the top of the bud.

2 Make 4 large buds. Pattern: On 1 wire, make 3 CL with 18 beads, 1 CL with 24 beads, and 3 CL with 18 beads. Leave 2 inches of bare wire on each side. Bring together the 2 ends and twist tightly. Bend the middle CL down over the top of the bud.

3 Make 9 petals for the back of each blossom. Pattern: ¾-inch-bead BF, RT, RB, complete 5 rows. Take a 7-inch piece of 26-gauge gold wire, bend it in half, and place it over the front of the basic row about one-third of the way from the top. Take the left end of the wire and pull it to the right side and the right end and pull it to the left side. The modified basic frame is ready. (See photo 1.)

4 For row 6, bring the beads two-thirds of the way up the left side and loop bare wire around the extended wire. (See photo 2.)

5 Finish row 6 by going up to the top basic and wrapping the wire. Start row 7 as you normally would. Bring the beaded wire down the right side to the extended wire, wrap completely around with the bare wire, and return to the top basic. You have completed rows 7 and 8. (See photo 3.)

6 Complete rows 9 and 10 on the left side of the modified BF. Repeat rows 7 through 10 for rows 11 to 14. Complete rows 15 and 16 on the right side of the petal. The spool wire will be at the top of the frame. Bring it down to the bare wire on the left side and twist with the bare wire. Reduce the bottom wire to 1. Clip the top basic wire and bend it to the backside of the petal. (See photo 4.)

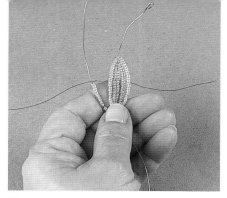

PHOTO 1. ADD A 7-INCH WIRE TO MODIFY THE BASIC FRAME.

PHOTO 2. ON ROW 6, LOOP THE BEADED WIRE AROUND THE MODIFIED FRAME.

PHOTO 3. ADD 2 MORE ROWS ON THE RIGHT SIDE OF THE MODIFIED FRAME.

PHOTO 4. CLIP THE TOP BASE WIRE AND BEND IT TO THE BACK.

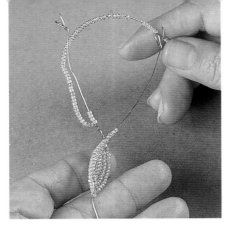

PHOTO 5. USE THE SPLIT BASIC TECHNIQUE TO MAKE THE FRONT PETAL.

7 See the instructions for the split basic technique in the Gold & White Orchid project on page 86. Make 9 petals for the front of each blossom. Pattern: Using the split-basic technique, make a 10-bead and include 8 beads in the loop. On the 10-bead BF, make a RT, RB for 5 rows. The top basic wire for this BF will become the part of the stem for the blossom. Do not clip it! On each side of the split loop, make a 4-bead BF, RT, RB for 5 rows. (See photo 5.)

8 Clip the basic wires for these 2 BFs and bend to the back. Leave about 4 inches of spool wire and clip. Add 1½ inches of pale green beads for the stamen on the bare wire and coil the top of the wire around a needle to lock the beads in place. Clip any excess wire from the stamen.

9 Make 8 small leaves for the stalk. Pattern: 1¼-inch-bead BF, PT, RB, 3 rows, reduce to 1 wire.

10 Make 8 large leaves for the stalk. Pattern: 1½-inch-bead BF, PT, RB, 5 rows, reduce to 1 wire.

11 Make 9 calyxes. Pattern: Make 7 CL, 15 beads each, leave 2 inches of bare wire on each side.

ASSEMBLING THE SNAPDRAGON BLOSSOMS

1 Place the front blossom petal on top of the front side (no wires showing) of the back petal. Twist the top basic wire of the front petal with the bottom loop wire of the back petal. (See photo 6.)

2 Bring the 2 sides of the back petal around the front petal. Pull the end wires of the modified basic frame under the two 4-bead BFs. Twist together the wires. Leave ⅜ inch and clip. (See photo 7.)

3 Coil the stamen to make it look squiggly. It will hide the wire from step 2. (See photo 8.)

4 Take the two 4-bead BFs, bend them slightly forward from the base, and then bend the tips to the back.

5 Attach the calyx under the blossom.

6 Mold the blossom to shape it.

ASSEMBLING THE SNAPDRAGON STALK

1 Attach 1 of the small buds to the top of the wrapped main stem wire.

2 With floral tape, add the other 2 small buds around the stem at ½ inch below the top bud.

3 Add the remaining buds and blossoms around the stem, clustering the blossoms closer together as you move down the stem.

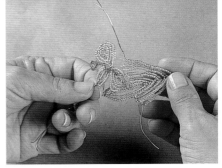

PHOTO 6. PLACE THE FRONT PETAL ON THE BACK PETAL.

PHOTO 7. BRING WIRES TO THE FRONT UNDER THE PETALS AND TWIST.

PHOTO 8. COIL STAMEN TO HIDE THE WIRE.

4 Make 4 bunches of 4 leaves each (vary the sizes) by wrapping the stems with floral tape. With floral tape, attach the leaves around the stem under the blossoms.

DESIGN TIP

Expand the snapdragon's lovely pastel palette with lavenders, yellows, and blues. Vary the size of the blossoms by adjusting the length of the basic row and the number of rows in the two petals.

Desktop Marigolds

E asy, easy—all the marigolds are made with simple continuous loops, the easiest of the four basic techniques. The small planter is the perfect size for a computer companion. Warning: if you display it at work, be prepared to make more— everyone else will want one, too!

DESIGN BY MELISSA ELLIS

Basic Technique

Continuous Loops (CL)

Marigold

1 blossom with 4 centers (small, medium, large, and extra-large)
4 leaves, with 3 leaflets each
1 calyx

What You Need for 1 Marigold (make 10 for the planter)

1 hank	11/0 yellow beads for small center
1 hank	11/0 orange beads for medium and large centers
1 hank	11/0 brown beads for extra-large center
1 hank	11/0 green beads for leaves and calyx
1 spool	26-gauge gold wire for inner and outer centers
1 spool	24 or 26-gauge green wire for leaves and calyx
1 piece	18-gauge wire for stem, cut to 8 inches, wrapped with floral tape
4 pieces	18-gauge wire, for secondary stems, cut to 1 inch

Floral clay
Dried Moss
Small container
Basic Flower-Making Kit

Making the Parts of the Marigold

1 Make 1 small yellow center. Pattern: Make 5 CL with 7 beads each. Leave 2 inches of bare wire on each side in this step and in the following steps, 2 through 5.

2 Make 1 medium orange center. Pattern: Make 7 CL with 11 beads each.

3 Make 1 large orange center. Pattern: Make 9 CL with 15 beads each.

4 Make 1 extra-large brown center. Pattern: Make 11 CL with 19 beads each.

5 Make the calyx. Pattern: Make 8 CL with 1 inch of beads each.

6 Make 4 small leaves. Pattern: Push 5 inches of beads up to within 3 inches of the knot on the end of the wire. Fold the beaded wire in half. Twist the beads together 2 or 3 times. Twist the bare wires together for 2 inches. Clip from the spool.

7 Make 4 medium leaves. Pattern: Push 6 inches of beads up to within 3 inches of the knot on the end of the wire. Fold, twist, and clip as you did in step 6 above.

8 Make 4 large leaves. Pattern: Push 7 inches of beads up to within 3 inches of the knot on the end of the wire. Fold, twist, and clip as you did in step 6 above.

Assembling the Marigold

1 Make a circle with the small center and twist the wires together. Place the small center at the tip of the wrapped stem wire and attach it with assembly wire.

2 Place the medium center under and around the small center and attach it with assembly wire.

3 Repeat step 2 with the large and extra-large centers and the calyx.

4 Wrap the stem with floral tape to cover the wires.

5 Make 4 clusters of 3 leaves each. Hold the end of a small, medium, and large leaf and wrap the stems together with floral tape. Attach to 1 of the 1-inch pieces of 18-gauge stem wire. (This will serve as a stem for planting.) Trim any wires from the leaves so they are even with the stem wire.

6 Work the clay with your hands to soften it, and press it into the container. Plant the marigolds and leaves. Cover with dried moss.

Design Tip

Have fun finding a variety of pretty and unusual containers in which to plant the marigolds. Small arrangements make terrific gifts for co-workers to brighten up their work areas.

Holiday Wreath Centerpiece

You'll never find a store-bought holiday wreath as beautiful as this one, or one that you'll show off with such pride year after year. The wreath—with its poinsettias, holly sprigs, pinecones, and clusters of leaves—uses more colors of beads than other projects. Three shades of green emphasize the different shapes and textures of the wreath's foliage. Two different tipping techniques make glittery pinecone decorations.

Basic Techniques

Basic Frame (BF)
Continuous Loops (CL)
Continuous Wraparound Loops (CWL)

Special Techniques

Tipping on the Loops

New Techniques

Tipping on the Edges

The Wreath

- 2 poinsettias (1 small, 1 large) with poinsettia leaves
- 2 holly sprigs with holly leaves and berries
- 2 hemlock pinecones
- 1 ponderosa pinecone
- 135 wreath leaves

Poinsettia

- 10 petals
- 1 center
- 3 leaves

WHAT YOU NEED FOR 1 POINSETTIA (LARGE OR SMALL)

2 hanks	11/0 deep red beads for petals
1 strand	11/0 yellow beads for center
1 hank	11/0 dark green beads for leaves
1 spool	24-gauge red wire for petals
1 spool	24-gauge green wire

Basic Flower-Making Kit

MAKING THE SMALL POINSETTIA

1 Make 5 small petals. Pattern: 1-inch-bead BF, PT, PB, 9 rows, reduce to 1 wire.

2 Make 5 large petals. Pattern: 1½-inch-bead BF, PT, PB, 11 rows, reduce to 1 wire.

3 Make 1 center. Pattern: 10 CL with 15 beads each. Leave 3 inches of bare wire on either end.

4 Make 3 poinsettia leaves. Pattern: 13-bead BF, PT, RB, 11 rows. On row 10, about one-third of the way from the bottom of the leaf, make a 7-bead loop. Twist completely around and continue another one-third of the

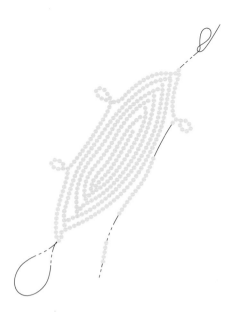

FIGURE 1. THE POINSETTIA LEAF HAS A 10-BEAD LOOP ONE-THIRD OF THE WAY FROM THE TOP AND ONE-THIRD FROM THE BOTTOM ON EACH OF THE LAST 2 ROWS.

PHOTO 1. THIS IS THE ASSEMBLED POINSETTIA.

way to the top, make another 7-bead loop, and twist that one completely, too. Finish the row. Make another 2 loops similarly placed on row 11. (See figure 1.)

MAKING THE LARGE POINSETTIA

1 Make 5 small petals. Pattern: 1¼-inch-bead BF, PT, PB, 9 rows, reduce to 1 wire.

2 Make 5 large petals. Pattern: 1¾-inch-bead BF, PT, PB, 11 rows, reduce to 1 wire.

3 Make 1 center. Pattern: 13 CL with 13 beads each. Leave 3 inches of bare wire on either end.

4 Make 3 poinsettia leaves. Pattern: 16-bead BF, PT, RB, 13 rows. On rows 12 and 13, repeat the loop and twist process in step 4 for the small poinsettia above OOO.

ASSEMBLING THE POINSETTIAS

1 Assemble each flower, 1 at a time, in the same way: Make the completed center by rolling the yellow center from its 1st loop into the 2nd, continuing with all the loops until you have a cluster of loops. Twist together the wires, making the stem. (See photo 1.)

2 Attach the small petals under the center.

3 Attach the large petals under the small petals.

4 Add the leaves under the large petals.

Holly Sprig

3 leaves
3 berries

WHAT YOU NEED FOR 1 HOLLY SPRIG

2 hanks	11/0 light green beads for leaves
1 hank	11/0 transparent red beads for berries
1 spool	24-gauge green wire for leaves
1 spool	26-gauge red wire for berries

Basic Flower-Making Kit

PHOTO 2. THE HOLLY LEAF USES SPOKES ON THE BASIC FRAME.

MAKING THE HOLLY LEAVES

1 Make 3 leaves. Pattern: 1¼-inch to 1½-inch-bead BF, PT, PB, 15 to 17 rows, reduce to 2 wires and twist.

2 Add natural-looking "spokes" by modifying the leaf frame with the following steps. One-third of the way up row 6 make the 1st spoke on the edge of the leaf with a 1-inch twist of bare wire. Push beads to the bottom of the twist, continue up the row to one-third from the top of the leaf, and twist more bare wire for the 2nd twist. Finish the row. Make twists on the opposite side of the leaf on row 7. (See photo 2.)

3 For row 8, bring the beads up the left side. Wrap bare wire around the 1st spoke you made in step 2. Take the beaded wire to the 2nd spoke and wrap bare wire around it, too. Take the beaded wire to the top basic wire and wrap it as you normally would. Proceed with row 9 as you did with row 8.

4 Continue for the remaining 6 to 8 rows, molding the leaf into its distinctive holly leaf shape as you go. When you have completed the leaf, wrap the spool wire around the base 2 or 3 times and clip the wire from the spool. Clip the top basic wire and bend it back to hide it. Clip the spokes, leaving about ⅛ inch, and bend them to the back of the leaf.

MAKING THE HOLLY BERRIES

1 Make 3 berries. Make a loop with 5 inches of beads and twist together the end wires.(See photo 3.)

2 Fold the beaded loop in half and thread the bare wires through the loop, making another loop.(See photo 4.)

3 Pull the wires through the bottom and then wrap the bottom wire onto itself. Mold the beaded part into a ball to resemble a berry.

ASSEMBLING THE HOLLY SPRIG

1 Hold together the bases of the three holly leaves. Place the berries on top of them. With nylon jaw-nose pliers, twist all the wires together. Wrap with floral tape.

PHOTO 3. START WITH A LOOP OF BEADS.

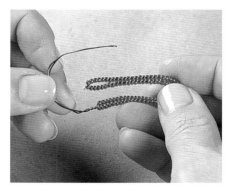

PHOTO 4. PULL THE WIRES THROUGH THE LOOP.

Hemlock Pinecone

19 scale sections (each has
4 different scale sizes, totalling
57 scales for each pinecone)

WHAT YOU NEED FOR
1 HEMLOCK PINECONE

2 hanks	11/0 transparent copper beads
1 spool	26-gauge gold or colored wire for pinecone scales

Brown floral tape
Basic Flower-Making Kit

MAKING THE HEMLOCK PINECONE SCALES (18 SECTIONS)

1 Make 1 section of 3 small scales. Pattern: 3 CWL, 2 loops each, beginning with a 10-bead loop. Leave 3 inches of bare wire on each side in this step and the following steps 2 through 4.

2 Make 3 sections of 3 medium scales. Pattern: 3 CWL, 2 loops each, beginning with a 14-bead loop.

3 Make 7 sections of 3 large scales. Pattern: 3 CWL, 2 loops each, beginning with a 16-bead loop.

4 Make 8 sections of 3 extra-large scales. Pattern: 3 CWL, 2 loops each, beginning with an 18-bead loop.

ASSEMBLING THE HEMLOCK PINECONE

1 Take the section of small scales and twist the wires together, forming a circle with the loops.

2 Place 1 section of medium scales underneath the small-scale section. Using nylon jaw-nose pliers, carefully twist together the wires. Add the remaining 2 medium-scale sections. Add the large and extra-large scale sections one by one so the extra-large sections are on the bottom of the cone. Twist the wire onto the stem with nylon jaw-nose pliers (or your fingers) as you add the sections.

3 Wrap the stem with brown floral tape.

Ponderosa Pinecone

38 scales

WHAT YOU NEED FOR
1 PONDEROSA PINECONE

2 hanks	11/0 bronze beads
1 hank	11/0 gold beads to shade the tips of the scales
1 spool	26-gauge gold wire

Brown floral tape
Basic Flower-Making Kit

MAKING THE PONDEROSA PINECONE

1 Make 1 center scale. Pattern: 3 CL with 2 inches of beads each, leave 3 inches of bare wire on each end. Tip the edges of the loops with gold (see instructions for tipping on the loops in the Fancy Japanese Iris project on page 70). Start with a 6-inch string of beads with the beads strung in the following sequence: ¾ inch bronze beads, ½ inch gold beads, 1 ½ inches bronze beads, ½ inch gold, 1 ½ inch bronze, ½ inch gold, ¾ inch bronze. Leave 3 inches of bare wire on each side, which will become the basis of the stem.

2 Make 3 small scales. Pattern: 4-bead BF, PT, RB, 5 rows, reduce to 1 wire. See the illustration and the instructions on tipping the edges on the basic frame on page 22. Tip the top one-third of the outer 2 rows of each small scale. You'll tip the last 2 rows of the remaining scales in steps 3 through 6 below in the same way. (See figure 2.)

3 Make 4 medium scales. Pattern: 5-bead BF, PT, RB, 5 rows, reduce to 1 wire. Tip the tops.

4 Make 10 large scales. Pattern: 6-bead BF, PT, RB, 7 rows, reduce to 1 wire. Tip the tops.

5 Make 10 extra-large scales. Pattern: 7-bead BF, PT, RB, 9 rows, reduce to 1 wire. Tip the tops.

6 Make 10 extra-extra-large scales. Pattern: 8-bead BF, PT, RB, 9 rows, reduce to 1 wire. Tip the tops.

FIGURE 2. TIP THE EDGES OF THE SCALES OF THE PONDEROSA PINE CONE WITH GOLD BEADS.

ASSEMBLING THE PONDEROSA PINECONE

1 Take the center scale (that you made in step 1 above) and, using the nylon jaw-nose pliers, twist together the wires. These twisted wires will become the stem of the pinecone.

2 Hold the 3 small scales under the center scale. With the pliers, tightly but carefully twist together all of the wires.

3 Add the remaining scales around the stem, gradually increasing the number and size of scales in each layer so the largest ones are on the bottom.

4 Cover the stem with brown floral tape.

5 Bend down the tips of the scales slightly so they look natural.

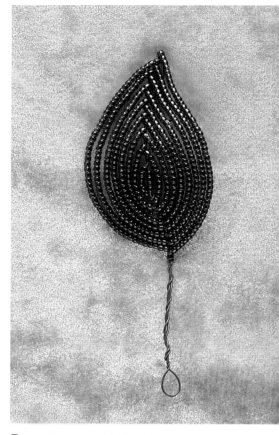

PHOTO 5. YOU'VE COMPLETED A LEAF FOR THE WREATH.

WHAT YOU NEED FOR THE 135 WREATH LEAVES

10 hanks	11/0 transparent green beads
1 package	24-gauge green paddle wire
1	wire wreath frame, 12-inch-diameter
Basic Flower-Making Kit	

MAKING THE WREATH LEAVES

1 Make 135 (or more) leaves in 3 different sizes. Pattern: 4-bead BF, PT, RB, reduce to 3 wires and twist. Make 35 or so leaves with 13 rows, 35 or so with 15 rows, and 65 with 17 rows. (See photo 5 on opposite page.)

2 Make 45 leaf clusters, each one with 3 leaves of various sizes. Wrap each cluster with floral tape.

ASSEMBLING THE TABLE WREATH

1 Attach each leaf cluster to the wreath frame with assembly wire. Layer the clusters so they overlap each other and look thick and full. (See photo 6.)

2 With assembly wire, attach and arrange the poinsettias, the pinecones, and the holly sprigs, as you like.

PHOTO 6. ADD CLUSTERS OF LEAVES TO THE WREATH.

Napkin Ring

Napkin rings make a lovely accent to your holiday table, especially when partnered with a holiday wreath centerpiece.

WHAT YOU NEED FOR 1 NAPKIN RING

3	holly leaves
3	berries
1 hank	11/0 green beads
1 spool	26-gauge wire
1	18-gauge stem wire
Basic Flower-Making Kit	

MAKING THE NAPKIN RING

1 Make 3 holly leaves and 3 berries according to the directions for the Holly Sprig on page 118.

2 String about 3 feet of green beads onto the 26-gauge wire.

ASSEMBLING THE NAPKIN RINGS

1 Curl the 18-gauge wire completely around a cylindrical object about 2 inches in diameter, such as a spice bottle or pill container, or another diameter that you want for the napkin rings. Clip the wire.

PHOTO 7. BEAD THE RING WITH BEADED WIRE.

2 Attach the 3 holly leaves and 3 berries to one end of the wire, and wrap assembly wire to secure. Wrap all the wires with floral tape.

3 Bead completely around the ring (see instructions on page 53). (See photo 7.)

4 Finish by wrapping beaded wire into a coil at the end and then, going the opposite direction, wrapping bare wire into a space between the beads.

WHEN NOT IN USE ON YOUR TABLE, THE WREATH LOOKS STUNNING AS A HANGING DECORATION. IT'S VERY HEAVY, SO USE A STURDY WALL FASTENER.

DESIGN TIP

Feel free to change the color of the wreath and the napkin rings. For a fancy wreath, make the leaves white and the poinsettias gold. Make the pinecones bigger by gradually increasing the number or size of the sections or scales. Add more or fewer of the flowers, leaves, and pinecones to suit your personal style.

NEW TECHNIQUE

TIPPING ON THE BASIC FRAME

Tipping a petal or a leaf made with a basic frame makes it look as if you dipped its top into a different color. Examples are the Ponderosa Pinecone in this project and the Glass House Dahlia on page 41. This technique is similar to outlining the last 2 rows of a petal described in the Anemone Accessory project on page 59, but instead of using a different color for the entire length of the last 2 rows, you'll use a different color only for sections of those rows.

1 When you are ready to begin tipping, estimate the amount of bare wire you need to complete the flower, and clip it from the spool.

2 Add a different color for the top one-third of the last even row and for the first one-third of the last odd row.

122   *The Art of French Beaded Flowers*

Fantasy Flowers

I picked a bunch of beads, put them in front of me, and just let this flower happen! It wasn't derived from anyone else's design, not even Mother Nature's.

After making many reality-based beaded flowers, you, too, might enjoy letting your artistic vision bloom into make-believe. There aren't any patterns for fantasy flowers—creativity and "why not?" are your only guides. Have fun!

1 Make petals with new bead and color combinations. (Making fantasy flowers is a wonderful way to use up leftover beads!) To add texture to the flower, I used a combination of bugle beads, 11/0 beads, and 8/0 beads. I alternated bugles and seed beads and used the larger seed beads at the top of the petal to create the little bumps. One blossom is pink and the other blue; both use size 8/0 lavender beads to provide consistency and continuity of color.

2 Experiment with shapes. Anything dramatic works—petals that are extra long or super ruffled, extravagant trumpet centers, leaves with quirky loops or points. The medium-sized bugle beads exaggerate the length of the petals in this flower. Even though it's necessary to put the beads on the wire one by one, the effect is wonderful and ultra-modern. I alternated a size 11/0 bead with a size 3/0 bugle bead for the first 7 rows of the petals. For the remaining rows, I alternated the size 8/0 and a bugle bead at the top of the petal. Both ends of the petals are pointed, and there are about 17 rows in each of the 5 petals. (See photo 1.)

3 Make dramatic centers. I wanted the center to look as if it were growing out of the flower. I made 5 rows of blue for one flower (pink for the other) and then began to add a little yellow at the base of the petal. I added a small amount of yellow beads at the beginning of all the even-numbered rows and at the end of the odd-numbered rows. The yellow was a bead-soup mix of many different yellow beads, including various sizes (6/0 to 12/0), shades, and finishes. (See photo 1.)

4 Make show-off stamens. There are 7 stamens in the center and each is made from a wire strung with bugle beads and a crystal at the top. I used assembly wire for the stamens so that after I put a seed bead above the crystal, I could hide the wire by weaving it into the crystal and a few bugle beads.

5 Make greenery as varied as the blossoms. This flower has two kinds of greenery—petals on a fairly tall stem and a twisted, loopy fern. It's nothing more than a very large simple loop (about 20 inches of beads) with an occasional crystal thrown in for a little glitz.

6 Forget gravity. Fantasy flowers don't have to abide by the rules of nature or even logic, so let them display themselves with abandon. Because the center of this flower was so heavy, I used the lacing technique (instructions page 54) to give the flower extra strength.

PHOTO 1. USE A COMBINATION OF BUGLE BEADS AND SEED BEADS TO CREATE FANTASY PETALS.

7 Linda Lindsey uses different approaches in her fantasy flowers. In her full-size arrangement on the opposite page, Linda gives her leaves equal billing with the flowers. For the leaves she uses a couple rows of bugle beads, changes to rows of seed beads, and then finishes up with more rows of bugles. In a bold departure from the traditional basic frame technique, the rows are deliberately spread apart, creating a light and airy effect. On one leaf, she adds a small simple loop at the top point. I've never seen a leaf like that, but it sure does look good in the arrangement!

8 The lilylike flower is a combination of seed beads and bugles. The stamens are a length of seed beads with 2 bugles, side by side, making the anther or the top of the stamens.

COLOR ADDS TO THE CHARM OF THIS FANTASY FLOWER—AN UNORTHODOX
COMBINATION OF BLUES, PURPLES, AND GREENS.

DESIGN BY LINDA LINDSEY

TO SET OFF SMALL FANTASY FLOWER
ARRANGEMENTS, PLANT THEM IN
A BEADED BASE.

DESIGN BY LINDA LINDSEY

WITH ITS EARTH AND NEUTRAL
TONES, THIS SMALL FANTASY
ARRANGEMENT COMPLEMENTS
ALMOST ANY COLOR SCHEME.

DESIGN BY LINDA LINDSEY

9 Loops play a large part in her tiny fantasy flower above right. A small red simple loop appears as a blossom, while a longer blue one has its edges tipped with gold beads. All the stems are twisted together so the arrangement almost looks like a clump of flowers that was pulled out of the ground.

10 In another small arrangement, at right, two large loops act as a filler or type of "greenery." Another leaf has an isolated loop off the tip. The neutral tones of the flower highlight the two large and silken beads that make up the flower center. Taken together, the flowers appear quite natural in a fantasy setting.

Acknowledgments

Thank you to everyone who, like beads on a string, played an essential part in the birth of this book:

Sandi Graves, for helping me find my first beaded flower book.

Linda Lindsey, my first beaded flower teacher, who taught me the basic frame.

Roberta Troeder, for her support, encouragement, and advice.

Dr. Thomas Graham, who rescued my bead career by repairing my hand when I broke it.

Ruth and Ralph, my fairy godparents, who shared their home where many of the flowers first saw the light of day.

Dennis Arnold, my florist and teacher, who taught me how to make flowers come alive.

Virginia Nathanson, who inspired and encouraged me to write a book.

The Beadedflower Group on the Internet, for sharing their wealth of knowledge.

My students, who continue to teach me.

My Dad, who always asked "How many beads in that flower?"

My siblings and instant messaging buddies, especially Mandy and Julia, who tolerated my long absences while I worked on the book.

My nephew, Brian, who at age 4, couldn't resist the bead spinner.

My great friend, DJ, who said, "You'll do it."

All the wonderful folks at Lark Books, especially:

Marcianne Miller, my editor, who tortured me mercilessly and pushed, pushed, pushed to convince me I really could write this book,

Stacey Budge, the incredible art director who turned my dream book into a reality beyond my dreams,

Keith Wright, the photographer whose magic sparkled every flower,

Jeannée Ledoux, the proofreader who lassoed all those errant commas,

Elisabeth B. Miller, the assistant who double-checked everything,

And, of course, to Alan, my husband and best friend, for hugs and wonderful dinners.

DESIGN BY ROSEMARY TOPOL

MELISSA ELLIS is a self-pro-claimed beaded flower fanatic, who has been making flowers since the mid-1990s. Melissa teaches beaded flower classes at bead stores in the Portland, Oregon, area and was excited to be accepted into the 2003 Bead Dreams show with her version of the Crown Imperial plant called Blooming Straight and Tall. She is well known for her jackets that are laden with embroidered butterflies and flowers and French-beaded corsages. She also loves to combine beaded flowers with holiday arrangements. Ms. Ellis lives in Vernonia, Oregon. ellis970@earthlink.net

LINDA LINDSEY has been beading since the 1970s. When her mother gave Linda a little picture frame with beaded flowers in it, she took it apart and re-created her own flowers, and she hasn't stopped beading since. She has taught a variety of beading courses, including French beaded flowers and beadweaving techniques. Linda truly brings the French bead flower-making technique into the 21st century, and specializes in whimsical and charming fantasy pieces. She worked at the Shepherdess bead shop in San Diego, California, for 10 years and now works at Lost Cities in the same city.
keben@cox.net

ROSEMARY TOPOL has been making beaded flowers since the late 1960s. She has won many awards for her beaded flower arrangements in local, national, and international competitions. She enjoys doing custom work for weddings, Bar and Bat Mitzvahs, and other occasions. She has produced a one-hour beginner's instructional videotape for the French beaded flower technique. Ms. Topol lives on Long Island, New York. Roe_topol@juno.com or http://www.geocities.com/roetopol

ROBERTA TROEDER, an avid beadweaver, started making French beaded flowers in the late 1960s. Her work has been exhibited at area craft shows, antique shops, and bead shops. She teaches French beaded flower-making for the Bead Society of Greater New York, the Craft Students League in New York, and has given demonstrations for many other groups. A stickler for detail and an advocate for tradition, Ms. Troeder is an inspiration and mentor to many new French beaded flower-makers. She lives in New Rochelle, New York. rstroeder@aol.com

Metric Conversions

WIRE GAUGE/DIAMETER

American Wire Gauge	Closest Metric Diameter in Millimeters (mm)
12	2.00 mm
14	1.50 mm
16	1.25 mm
18	1.00 mm
20	.75 mm
22	.64 mm
23	.57 mm
24	.50 mm
26	.41 mm
28	.32 mm
30	.25 mm
32	.20 mm
34	.16 mm

WEIGHT

½-kilo bag of beads weighs
1.1 pound

LENGTH

Inches	Approx. Metric Measurement
¼	6.0 mm
½	1.3 cm
¾	1.9 cm
1	2.5 cm
1¼	3.2 cm
1½	3.8 cm
2	5.0 cm
2½	6.4 cm
3	7.6 cm
3½	8.9 cm
4	10.2 cm
4½	11.4 cm
5	12.7 cm
5½	14.0 cm
6	15.2 cm
6½	16.5 cm
7	17.8 cm
7½	19.0 cm
8	20.3 cm
8½	21.6 cm
9	22.9 cm
9½	24.1 cm
10	25.4 cm

Index